Science for Seniors
Hands-On Learning Activities

Gloria Hoffner, BA, ADC, AC-BC
Winner of 2010 NCCAP Best Practice Award

Idyll Arbor, Inc.

39129 264th Ave SE, Enumclaw, WA 98022 (360) 825-7797

Idyll Arbor Editor: Chris Blaschko

ISBN: 9781882883776

Printed in the United States of America

Library of Congress Cataloging-in-Publication Data

Dedication

To my family for believing in me.
My parents — Gloria and George Hoffner
My sisters — Helen Hoffner and Nancy Catania
My husband — Jim McCall
Our sons — Richard and Stephen Hoffner-McCall

Acknowledgements

Nancy Newman, Activity Director at Sterling Healthcare and Rehabilitation Center in Media, PA, for allowing me to create Science for Seniors.

Kelley Smith, Sterling Activity Assistant, for creating wonderful props and materials for Science for Seniors.

Sterling Activity Department members Gina Clements, Sharyn Carr, Joan Di Sciullo, Carroll Erricson, Joyce McCormick, Inna Melnyk, Louise Smith, Judy McNeill, Jakena Costen, and Jean Walker for support and help with the program. Also thanks to Frank Marchese, general manager for his enthusiasm, the Sterling kitchen and maintenance departments for program supplies.

Andy Sol of the Delaware County Institute of Science, Media, PA. Chris Brust, physics consultant residing in Baltimore, MD.

And my best friend Mary Anne Janco who supported my writing and when I doubted my ability to finish this book said, "You will."

Contents

Introduction

Science for Seniors is based on one belief: we are never too old to learn. History is full of individuals who have never stopped learning and increasing their knowledge. Some of these renowned figures include Anna Mary Robertson Moses, who is better known as Grandma Moses. Grandma Moses learned to paint in her 70s and became an acclaimed artist with worldwide exhibits. Actress Betty White, who in 2010 launched a new television series, won her sixth Emmy award, designed her own line of fashion clothing, and became an author at the age of 88.

Brian May, a household name for Boomers, was the lead singer and songwriter for the rock band Queen. He returned to college and earned a PhD in astrophysics at the age of 61. After graduating, he published a book, *A Survey of Radial Velocities in the Zodiacal Dust Cloud,* and at age 63 he became Chancellor at Liverpool's John Moors University.

What these individuals' accomplishments demonstrated, science is now proving. Clive A. Wilson, author of *No One Is Too Old to Learn: Neuroandragogy: A Theoretical Perspective on Adult Brain Functions and Adult Learning,* discusses how adults can learn new concepts and sharpen their minds throughout life. He states that this is possible because the brain plasticity still occurs late in life. Even more interesting is that Wilson points out humans may be able to experience new brain cell growth as we age, if we continue the lifelong process of learning. His book also makes an argument for the theory of a possible delay of Alzheimer's disease in people who continue to learn.

The benefits of lifelong learning are demonstrated in the book *The Brain That Changes Itself: Stories of Personal Triumph from the Frontiers of Brain Science* by Norman Doidge. In his book he states, "The more education we have, the more socially and physically active we are, and the more we participate in mentally stimulating activities, the less likely we are to get Alzheimer's disease or dementia."

"Not all activities are equal in this regard. Those that involve genuine concentration — studying a musical instrument, playing board games, reading and dancing — are associated with a lower risk for dementia" (pp. 255-256).

Doige reports that education is not a cure-all for the crippling diseases of Alzheimer's and dementia, but he says the possibility that brain stimulation can delay these conditions is "very promising."

Gene D. Cohen, author of *The Mature Mind,* cites a University of California — Berkeley study by Marion Diamond that demonstrated that the brains of young and old rats both grew in response to new stimulation and learning environments.

Cohen also reported on the findings of Joseph LeDoux, a behavioral neuroscientist at New York University, who found that new learning experiences boost the development of brains and improve the information processing and memory storage in mid-life and older. Cohen reminds his readers, "Our brains are deeply connected to our bodies via nerves, hormones, and the immune system. Anything that stimulates the brain, reduces stress and promotes a more balanced emotional response will trigger positive changes in the body" (p 176).

Cohen ends his book with, "We need not succumb to difficulties, nor need we accept the myths that still exist about growing old. Nature endows us with the mental potential we need to improve our health, our relationships and our lives" (p 18).

Author's story

In October 2007, I created Science for Seniors as an activity program to celebrate the 50th anniversary of Sputnik with residents at Sterling Healthcare and Rehabilitation in Media, PA. Nancy Newman, Activity Director, approved the idea and Kelley Smith, Activity Assistant, created wonderful props for the program.

The success of this event resulted in the creation of a monthly science program at Sterling. Those programs led to this book with the goal of helping activity departments in many venues including retirement communities, assisted living facilities, skilled nursing care homes, and adult day centers. This book will help create educational, fun, and engaging science programs for clients at these facilities.

Science for Seniors is designed to involve residents in a hands-on learning experience with new discoveries about the world. Each chapter offers a way to combine the latest scientific discoveries with residents' memories, discussions of current events, and taking part in the fun of trivia.

An example from Chapter 3 is the BP Gulf Coast Oil Disaster. Residents discuss the impact of the spill and those who have lived or visited the affected areas tell the group about their experiences. After watching a video on the process of drilling for oil, the residents take part in an experiment illustrating natural ways of cleaning oil spills.

Science for Seniors programs can also be sparked by a resident's fond memory. A resident spoke of her train travels on the famous Horseshoe Curve of Pennsylvania. Built into a hillside in 1854 and called an engineering marvel, the curve located about five miles west of Altoona is part of a working rail line and a popular tourist site.

The train science program includes a model train and an experiment — using only a pinwheel and a teakettle — to demonstrate the steam powered engines that originally carried trains around Horseshoe Curve.

When Sterling's activity department learned a resident was a WWII veteran who had served on a submarine, the Science for Seniors experiment focused on how submarines work with a lesson on the density of water, found in Chapter 6.

Science for Seniors can expand residents' knowledge of the United States and the world by demonstrating what happens during an earthquake, a volcanic eruption, the possible future reshaping of the globe due to global warming, and even what scientists predict about the end of the world.

With hands-on demonstrations using every day items from plastic wrap to cooking oil, Science for Seniors gives residents a new insight into how the world works. Through experiments and museum loans, Science for Seniors also encourages residents to remember trips such as seaside vacations, while holding an artifact from the ocean in their hands and learning new facts about the water.

My own interest in science goes back to 1967 when, in sixth grade, I wrote to NASA and asked what courses I needed to study to be an astronaut. In reply, NASA sent me a form letter outlining courses and then in blue ink at the bottom of the letter wrote, "Of course women are not allowed to be astronauts." NASA should have said, "No American women" as the Russians had placed a woman in space prior to my letter!

I went on to study journalism, my second love after science, and after earning a degree from Temple University, I spent over 30 years working as a newspaper reporter. I covered a variety of subjects, mostly education, but I was thrilled whenever I could report on astronomy. I enrolled in astronomy graduate classes in the 1990s with an eye on earning my masters and perhaps teaching science.

Midway through this degree I met with a career counselor to plan my science future. She politely told me that when I graduated at age 53, I would be, "too old for any school to hire you as a starting science teacher." Shortly after her comments, the financial support for the classes through my job ended.

Life was about to find another path for me: a new career in science which began with my love of music. I play baritone horn in the Chichester Alumni Community Band and each month we play a concert at a local long-term care facility. I met many activity directors and expressed my interest in entering the field.

While still working full time as a reporter at *The Philadelphia Inquirer*, in 2006 I took a part-time job, a few hours a week, at a local nursing home. I loved being with the residents! I enrolled in an activity director course and in January 2007 I left the newspaper.

I opened my own business, Guitar with Gloria & Science for Seniors. I play music and lead sing-a-longs at retirement centers, nursing homes, assisted living facilities, adult day centers, senior clubs, and community events. I also bring the interactive Science for Seniors programs to these communities.

Since 2007, I have seen the monthly Science for Seniors program encourage participation among residents who shy away from facility parties and shun bingo. I've seen a woman who rarely leaves her room sit mesmerized by images from the Hubble telescope and a discussion of exoplanets. I've listened as a resident who rarely speaks suddenly spoke up and surprised her fellow residents with her scientific knowledge. And time after time, I witness residents leaving the science program saying, "That was so interesting." and "I never knew that." and "That was cool." And always, "I learn so much coming to these programs."

In 2010 the Science for Seniors program was the first place winner of the National Certification Council of Activity Professionals' Best Practice Award. Since 2010 I've written a monthly column, "Science for Seniors," for *Creative Forecasting Magazine* and since 2011 an activities column for the website About.com. I've spoken at national and statewide activity professional conventions and present workshops on Science for Seniors.

It is my hope and my goal that the ideas in this book will enable you to help your residents experience the joy of scientific discovery through Science for Seniors.

Let the adventure begin!

References

Cohen, Gene D. 2006. *The Mature Mind: The Positive Power of the Aging Brain*. Jackson, TN: Basic Books.

Doidge, Norman. 2007. *The Brain That Changes Itself: Stories of Personal Triumph from the Frontiers of Brain Science*. New York: Viking.

May, Brian. (2010, August 6). Brian May with Terry Gross interview. NPR radio. Retrieved August 7, 2010, from BrianMay.com

Wilson, Clive A. 2006. *No One Is Too Old to Learn*. Bloomington, IN: iUniverse, Inc.

Chapter 1 — Getting Started

Science for Seniors involves audience participation! Hold your science program in a large room with a television and a DVD/VHS player. You will need a table at the front of the room on which to place the items needed for your science program. If possible, also have a cart on which you can bring the experiments and demonstrations to audience members as needed.

Check materials needed! Purchase supplies, order library books, videos, and DVDs in advance of the scheduled program to assure timely arrival and use. If possible, arrange a meeting with your local library reference librarians. Tell them about your program and allow them to help you select from available local and interlibrary loan materials.

Ask local clubs, government programs, museums, and schools for loans of items such as animal pelts, seashells, rocks, fossils, slide shows, and even guest speakers.

Rehearsing is a must! Always test your experiment before working with the residents. You may need to adjust one ingredient or allow more time than you expected. Some of the experiments require growing plants, freezing ice cubes, etc. Always allow the time necessary for a successful experiment.

Arrange participation! Prior to the program ask a resident if he or she would like to help with Science for Seniors. Based on a resident's skills and abilities, have the resident add the ingredients for a volcano model, add salt for the water density experiment, or call the dog to the table for the animal senses demonstration. Residents may be invited to talk about how their past experiences relate to the program topic. Example: a resident may have been an electrician or worked for a power company, another may have collected seashells from around the world, and still another may have taught physics.

Ask residents for new topics! Always end a program by asking residents to suggest ideas for the next program. They may have always wondered why migrating birds fly in formation or how magnets work. One resident's suggestion usually prompts many similar comments and interests.

A Science for Seniors Program Has Five Parts

Each of the five parts of a Science for Seniors program adds to the total experience. The participants get a brief introduction to the topic. Trivia helps raise interest in the topic. Playing a video or having guest speakers is a way to provide a lot of information — and you might learn something, too. The hands-on demonstration or experiment brings the topic home by providing an activity right there in your facility. The follow-up allows residents to share their personal stories about the topic of the experiment. Let's take a look at each of the parts of the program.

✐ Give a brief explanation to the audience

Example: Today we are going to discuss the formation of the Earth. The Earth is one of eight planets in our solar system which obit around a single sun. The Earth is the third planet from the sun and the only one known to have life. The solar system formed about 4.6 billion years ago. It is part of the Milky Way Galaxy. The Milky Way is home for our sun and over 100 billion other stars. It is spiral-shaped like a pinwheel and our solar system is located in an outer arm.

♯ Include trivia facts

Easy

"What are the names of the eight planets?"
Answer: Mercury, Venus, Earth, Mars, Jupiter, Saturn, Uranus, and Neptune.

Challenging

"Which planet rotates on its side?"
Answer: Uranus, the third largest planet in the solar system, orbits with its axis almost level with the sun. Scientists believe this may be the result of Uranus' collision with another orbiting object sometime during its early history.

Bonus Round

"Why is Pluto no longer a planet?"
When Pluto was discovered in 1930 it was considered a planet. Then at the start of the 21st century, astronomers discovered other objects at the edge of our solar system, a region called Kuiper Belt. These objects, some larger than Pluto and also with moons, were classified along with Pluto as dwarf planets.

♯ Video

Show a video on the topic. There are many sources of science educational videos. The public showing of educational videos, such as Public Broadcasting System productions, is permitted as follows: "Products sold through the regular Shop PBS site are cleared for at-home, personal entertainment purposes only. While limited use of these programs in schools may be acceptable under federal copyright law, the programs must be used in face-to-face teaching settings." Further details available at: http://www.pbs.org/teachers/copyright/faqs.html#who

1) Begin with the selection of free or low cost videos at the library.
2) Video stores and video vending machines provide low cost DVDs.
3) Netflix: This is a DVD subscription service which offers a wealth of science videos for a low monthly fee. The service sends videos via the mail with unlimited return time. Netflix members may also

stream videos via computers, Wii systems or a Netflix device. Further information is available at Netflix.com.

4) Amazon.com and ShopPBS.org are examples of online locations to purchase science videos.

5) Always preview the video for length and content. A DVD series or lengthy DVDs can be shown in parts, as needed.

IV Experiment and/or demonstration

Put the trivia and video information into action. Examples: Create a table top volcano model that *explodes* by adding baking soda, red food coloring, water, and vinegar. Demonstrate the density differences between fresh and salt water with an egg, as explained in a later chapter in this book. Here are some things you should do with every experiment:

1) Always ask the residents to guess what they think will happen in the experiment. Example: Will the egg float or sink? Why did it float or sink?

2) Have a resident/residents participate. Example: Let one resident be the sun by holding a flashlight as a second resident stands in for Earth by walking around (orbits the sun) to demonstrate how, when, and where the sunlight strikes the planet, which results in the change of seasons on the Earth.

3) Always let the residents feel the experiment whenever possible. Bring the cart with the experiment to residents who cannot see the experiment at the front of the room. Examples: Put the residents' hands on the slime resulting from an egg immersed in salt water, the smooth inside of a seashell polished by ocean waves, or the grooves in a fossil.

4) Explain the science behind the experiment. Example: The plastic wrap filled with a half-inch of cooking shortening demonstrates how a polar bear's thick under-skin layer protects the bear from the freezing cold arctic waters.

5) Take photos or videos of the science program to post at your facility. Show families the variety of activities the residents enjoy. Share science program information with local news media.

✓ Discussion and Follow-up

Engage the residents in conversation about the topic. Example: Did they ever see a live volcano? Did they ever ride a steam-powered locomotive?

Provide further information on the topic. Example: Have available a few books or magazines on the program topic discussed. *National Geographic* magazines and/or books are available from the library, usually for a loan of one to two weeks. The county ombudsman may also supply books when requested by a retirement community. Audio books for the visually impaired are available on a wide range of topics.

As residents exit the program, ask for feedback. What did they like? What surprised them? What topics would they like to see in the future? Welcome suggestions for the next program. Example: A resident wanted to learn more about wild animals and another asked for a program on dinosaurs. Always have some topic suggestions to offer the residents to vote on for the next program just in case no one offers an idea or the resident suggested idea cannot be accomplished in the time period before the next scheduled science program.

Always tease residents with a tidbit of next month's program. For example: Next month the experiment includes a demonstration on how spiders keep from sticking to their webs!

Chapter 2 — Animals

Animals have been companions of humans since the dawn of history, from dogs to horses and every animal in between. So is it any wonder that humans have dedicate themselves to discovering all that they can about these animals? In this chapter we will learn about left- and right-pawed cats, the amazing noses of dogs and sharks among many other entertaining and thrilling subjects. This is a chapter you won't want to miss!

Birds

Introduction

Looking up into the sky at the graceful flight of a bird, or listening to the sweet sounds of birdsong, and even watching in amazement as a bird constructs a nest strand by strand are pleasant pastimes for humans.

Birds are not the first creatures to take flight across the lands and oceans of the Earth. The first winged creatures were insects. These buzzing life forms had exclusive use of the skies for about 300 million years. Next came winged dinosaurs and finally, around 150 million years ago, came the arrival of birds.

There are about 9,000 species of birds in the world today. The definition of a bird is not its flight, wings, or eggs. All birds share one common trait — feathers. The feathers keep a bird warm and help with in-flight steering. The color of a bird's feathers can protect a bird from a predator as well as help the bird attract a mate.

A bird's temperature is seven to eight degrees hotter than a human. Birds do not sweat. Three quarters of the air a bird breathes is used to cool the body.

There are between one and two billion birds living on the planet and over 40 million pet birds in the United States. Scientists believe birds are the descendents of dinosaurs. This is based in part on the Archaeopteryx, a dinosaur that lived about 150 million years ago. Similar in size to a chicken, the Archaeopteryx had feathers and could fly.

Trivia

Easy
Name a bird that does not fly.
Answer: Penguin, ostrich, or emu.

Challenging
What bird eats twice their weight in nectar each day and produces the world's smallest egg?
Answer: Hummingbird.

Bonus Round
Name some birds that can fly close to 200 miles per hour.
Answer: Doves, falcons, and sandpipers.

Video

If possible seek out a local bird watching club for a video, slide show, or even a guest speaker for this science program. The club or a museum may be able to provide sample bird eggs and nests.

The Life of Birds — National Geographic — three volume set on DVD.

Birds, Birds, Birds! An Indoor Birdwatching Field Trip — Produced by
    John Feith — DVD.

Audubon Society's Videoguides to Birds of North America. — PBS —
    two DVD set.

Experiment: What makes an eggshell hard?

Materials

- Three eggs — fresh or hard boiled
- Two cups of vinegar
- Two clear plastic containers large enough to hold one egg and one cup of vinegar

Process

Prior to the experiment:
Place one egg in one of the vinegar-filled containers 24 hours before the class and the second egg in another container 12 hours before the class. Leave the third egg unaltered, this egg will be used as a comparison to the other two eggs during the class.

During the experiment:
Set up your experiment prior to the class and have the two eggs which are in the vinegar covered with a cloth so they are not visible to

the residents. Allow the residents to handle the egg which was not put in the vinegar. Ask the residents what they think will happen when an egg is put into a cup of vinegar.

Remove the cloth and allow the residents to see the two eggs in the vinegar. Point out the bubbles which are coming off of the eggs. Remove the egg that has been in the vinegar for 12 hours and allow the residents to feel the softness as well as the slime on the egg — from the dissolving carbon. Next, remove the egg that was in the cup of vinegar for 24 hours and allow the residents to feel the softness of that egg.

Continuing the experiment:

If possible, leave the two eggs which were in the vinegar in a public and undisturbed location. Leave one egg in the open air and the second one in the cup of vinegar. The residents can feel the shell of the egg in the open air as it re-hardens. Meanwhile, the egg that remains in vinegar will continue to dissolve until there is no shell left.

Science behind the Experiment

As the softened eggs sit out in the air they will become hard again. This is because the calcium remaining in the shells pulls carbon from the carbon dioxide in the air and thus rehardens the shells. Place these eggs in a common area the day after the science program and allow the residents to stop and examine the rehardened eggs shells.

Egg shells are hard because they contain calcium carbonate. Vinegar is acetic acid. When the eggs are placed in the vinegar the resulting chemical reaction releases carbon dioxide — the gas seen escaping as bubbles rising from the eggs. The shells become soft when carbon is removed.

Experiment References

Kidzone. 2010. Soft Shelled Eggs Science Experiment. Retrieved May, 28, 2010. http://www.kidzone.ws/science/egg.htm.

Discussion

- Did anyone ever have a pet bird?
- Did anyone ever find a bird's nest or discover a freshly hatched egg?
- Did anyone ever live on a farm and raise chickens?

Further Reading Suggestions

Alsop, Fred J. 2001. *Smithsonian Handbooks: Birds of North America —
    Eastern Region*. New York: DK Adult.
Dunn, Jon L. and Jonathan Alderfer. 2006. *National Geographic Field
    Guide to Birds of North America*, Fifth Edition. Washington, DC:
    National Geographic.
Johnson, Jinny. 2003. *1000 Things You Should Know About Birds*.
    Broomall, PA: Mason Crest Publishers.

References

Learner.org. 2010. American Robin. Retrieved August 11, 2010.
    www.learner.org/jnorth/tm/robin/EggstraEggstra.html.
Watson, Jane Werner. 1981. *Dinosaurs and Other Prehistoric Reptiles*.
    New York: Golden Press.

Migrating Birds

Introduction

The sight of migrating birds in flight is a common event in areas of the planet that experience a change in seasons. Birds do not migrate simply for warmer weather. In the past, scientists believed that migrating birds sought fresh supplies of fruit growing in warm weather locations. This was studied in 2007 by W. Alice Boyle, an adjunct lecturer at the University of Arizona in Tucson's department of ecology and evolutionary biology, and by Courtney J. Conway, a UA assistant professor of natural resources and a research scientist with the U.S. Geological Survey.

Boyle and Conway studied 379 species of New World flycatchers, from a suborder of *Tyranni*, which are one of the largest groups of New World birds. They found food scarcity predicted the habits of migrating birds. It did not matter if the birds were seeking bugs or nectar; they traveled in search of an ample supply of food.

Flocking birds, such as Canadian geese, can travel from Canada to Mexico during winter to spring migration. In the process they can reach speeds of up to 60 miles per hour at up to 8,000 feet. These birds can fly for up to 16 hours without a rest and can also fly at night.

Non-flocking birds, such as the North American bald eagle, also travel to seek new food sources. Large hunting birds, such as the eagle, tend to be independent. Eagles, however, do stay with the same mate for life.

Trivia

Easy

Name a bird that migrates.

Answer: Sandhill cranes migrate from Alaska and Canada to U.S. southern states and Mexico. There are many other possibilities.

Challenging

How many eggs does each bird produce?

Answer: It depends on the bird. Chickens are bred to lay an egg every day. It takes 21 days for a chicken egg to hatch. Robins lay about four eggs per nesting. It takes 12 to 14 days for robin eggs to hatch.

Bonus Round

What is the smallest bird?

Answer: The male bee hummingbird weighs 0.056 ounces and is 2.75 inches in length — his bill and tail are half his total body length. This bird lives in Cuba.

Video

Winged Migration — Sony Pictures — DVD, 2005.
Nature: Birds — PBS — DVD, 2003.
The Life of Birds — BBC Productions — DVD set, 2002.

Experiment: Why do geese fly in formation?

Materials

- 8½" x 11" sheets of paper (one or more per resident)
- A large upright fan or a box fan that can be placed on a table

Process

Assist the residents in making simple paper birds.

1) The first step is to take an 8½" x 11" piece of paper and cut it so that you have a square. This is done by folding the top corner of the paper over until it meets the edge of the opposite corner. Create a crease and cut the remaining paper off.

2) Open the newly formed square and create a crease running in the opposite direction. The paper should now have four triangles.

3) Flip the paper over so that the paper tents upwards. Fold the paper in half so that you have two rectangles. Unfold it, do the same in the other direction. You should now have eight triangles.

4) Next, bring the four corners of the paper together. Flatten the paper. You should now have only two triangles visible from either side.
5) Set the paper so that the opening on the paper is on the top. Take one corner of the paper and fold it so that it is even with the center crease. Do this for the other three corners as well. This should give you a kite shape.
6) While the paper is still in the kite shape, fold the top part (where the opening is) down so that you once more have a triangular shape. Fold it to both sides.
7) Unfold the top so you once more have a kite shape and unfold the four corners so you once more have a square.
8) Taking only the top corner of the opening, pull it back using the crease from step 6 as the folding point. Crease the paper. Do the same to the other side. You should have a triangle shape now.
9) Position the triangle so that the split half of the bird is on the bottom. Fold both splits up, at a slight angle (these will become the head and tail).
10) Unfold both sides. Starting on the right side, unfold the right side, you should still have a triangle, one side will have more layers than the other.
11) Fold the "head" up using the creases you made the first time you folded them. Fold the right edge back over. This should put the "head" between the two wings. Do the same for the other side.
12) Next take the wings and fold them down at an angle away from the head. The bottom on the wing should be even with the bottom of the bird. Do this on both sides.
13) Lastly, make a beak on the bird by folding part of the paper down.

Next, line up the residents holding the paper birds in a V-shape as if they were migrating birds. Turn the large fan towards the paper birds.

Science behind the Experiment
The residents will feel the air flowing over the paper birds just as migrating birds feel the air currents when flying in V formation. This is so each bird can use the up-wash air from the neighboring bird as extra wind and a little extra lift, thus saving the energy of the birds in the

formation. The heartbeat of a bird at rest is about 400 beats per minute. In flight; their heartbeat becomes 1000 beats per minute.

Experiment References
Created by Gloria Hoffner.

Discussion

- Who has watched birds flying in formation?
- Who has visited a bird sanctuary?
- Who fed wild birds at a park or lake?

Further reading suggestions

Gibson, Graeme. 2005. *The Bedside Book of Birds: An Avian Miscellany*. New York: Nan A. Talese.

Ogbum, Charlton. 1976. *The Adventure of Birds*. New York: Morrow.

Yow, John. 2009. *The Armchair Birder: Discovering the Secret Lives of Familiar Birds*. Chapel Hill: University of North Carolina Press.

References

Sandhill Crane Migration. 2010. Retrieved August 24, 2010. www.sandhillcranemigration.com.

Science Daily. 2007. Why Do Birds Migrate? Retrieved August 7, 2010. www.sciencedaily.com/releases/2007/03/070302082310.htm.

Dogs

Introduction

Dogs have been partners with humans for more than 130,000 years. Scientists believe all dogs are descended from wolves and that the first wolf found her/his way into a human camp when seeking shelter from the elements.

Humans domesticated the wolves that evolved into dogs. Archeologists believe the first domesticated dogs were in Asia. As people moved about the globe, dogs went with them.

The many types of dogs are a result of human breeding for specific useful traits such as hunting and herding dogs. Dogs have been bred for agricultural uses and later, as people moved into cities, dogs were bred as household pets.

In the United States the most popular breeds of dogs are Labrador retriever, Yorkshire terrier, German shepherd, golden retriever, beagle, dachshund, boxer, poodle, Shih Tzu, and miniature schnauzers. There are about 74 million dogs in the United States. The worldwide count is difficult because dogs have many uses in the world. In some countries dogs are bred and used for their fur, as labor, and even as food.

In hearing, dogs have an advantage over people. They can hear sounds with frequencies as low as 16 to 20 Hz and as high as 70,000 to 100,000 Hz. Humans can hear in a range of 20 to 70 Hz for the low sounds and 20,000 Hz for high sounds.

Dogs can also recognize the location of a sound faster than humans. The average 18 or more muscles in dogs' ears allow them to tilt, rotate, and raise or lower their ears to rapidly pinpoint a sound. Dogs with straight, pointed ears hear better than those with floppy ears.

Dogs do not see the full spectrum of colors seen by humans; rather they see shades of purple and yellow. The dog's retina has rods which see in shades of gray, while humans see in color. By seeing only in gray, dogs can see in less light than humans and detect motion faster.

Trivia

Easy

What is meant by a three-dog night?

Answer: A night so cold that to stay warm you should sleep with three dogs.

Challenging

Where does the expression, "barking up the wrong tree" come from?

Answer: Old English saying for dogs that are tricked to gather and bay around a tree base by a raccoon that has jumped to another tree. Raccoons are the wild creatures that are best at fooling dogs

Bonus Round

What are the smartest dog breeds?

Answer: According to the American Kennel Club: Border collie, poodle, German shepherd, golden retriever, Doberman pincher, Shetland sheepdog, Labrador retriever, Papillion, rottweiler, and Austrian cattle dog.

Video

Nature: Dogs — Questar Video — DVD, 2003.

The World of Dogs — Columbia River Entertainment Group — DVD, 2007.

NOVA — Dogs and More Dogs — WGBN Boston — DVD, 2004.

You may be able to obtain a video from the local 4-H clubs, a canine association, or even the Police Department's K-9 division, as they use such videos when presenting talks at schools and community events.

Experiment: Can dogs detect odors humans miss?

Materials

- Two clean glass jars
- ½ cup of meat juice
- Water
- Sunlight
- A friendly dog
- Marker

Process

Prior to the experiment:

Mark the jars A and B. Swirl meat juice in jar A until it coats the sides.

Rinse jar A with water only and place jar it in the sunlight for one or more days. The sun and water will reduce the residual smell of meat in the jar.

During the experiment:

The following day bring both jars and the dog to the Science for Seniors program. Ask residents to smell both jars and guess which one had meat juices.

Next place the jars in front of the dog. The dog should sniff both but linger and maybe lick the jar that formerly held the meat juice.

Science behind the Experiment

Dogs' senses are different from humans. Dogs have over 200 million scent cells while humans have a mere five million scent cells. After the dog has made her/his decision on the jars, let additional residents try the same test. Sometimes the residents will get it right, but it may be because they are smelling the scent of the dog that just licked the jar.

Experiment References

Docstoc.com. 2010. Retrieved June 11, 2010.

www.docstoc.com/docs/22461514/Dogs-Sense-of-Smell.

Discussion

- Ask who was surprised they could not tell the difference in the jars.
- Have residents talk about their own dogs.
- Who has a funny story about their dog?

Further reading suggestions

Arts and Entertainment Network. 1998. *Big Dogs, little dogs: The World of Our Canine Companions*. New York: GT Pub.

Glover, Harry. 1970. *The Book of Dogs*. New York: Viking Press.

Johnson, Bruce and McKay, Sindy. 2009. *About Dogs*. San Anselmo, CA: Treasure Bay, Inc.

References

Amazing Dog Facts. 2010. Retrieved August 5, 2010. http://www.funshun.com/amazing-facts/dog-animal-facts.html.

Butler, Joy. 2006. Interesting Facts about Our Canines. Retrieved August 5, 2010. http://www.suite101.com/content/fundogfacts-a1171.

Dog Facts. 2010. Retrieved July 28, 2010. www.dogfacts.org/hearing-dog-facts.htm.

Evolution. 2010. Library: Evolution of the Dog. Retrieved July 12, 2010. http://www.pbs.org/wgbh/evolution/library/01/5/l_015_02.html.

Kearl, Mary. 2010. Ten Human Foods Dogs Can Eat. Retrieved July 29, 2010. www.pawnation.com/2010/07/28/10-human-foods-dogs-can-eat/?icid=main/main/dl3.

Mackie, Nicole. 2010. How Dogs Use Their Senses. K-9 Magazine. Retrieved July 12, 2010. http://www.k9magazinefree.com/k9_perspective/iss6p21.shtml.

Cats

Introduction

The history of domestic cats begins about 4,000 years ago when the ancient Egyptians used cats to kill mice and rats that were invading food storage sites. Egyptians worshiped cats as gods and goddesses and gave the death penalty to anyone who killed a cat.

Domesticated cats spread to Italy and then throughout Europe. The Pilgrims brought cats to America.

There are 36 breeds of cats around the world. The most popular cat worldwide is the Siamese. Cats are the most popular house pet in the United States, where about 37 percent of households have at least one cat, and 35 percent have two or more cats. The most popular breed in America is the Moggie, a non-pedigree domestic cat.

Cats have 230 bones, 24 more than a human. They have the largest eye to body size ratio of any mammal and can see six times better than a human.

Cats living outdoors have a life expectancy of about three to five years. Indoor cats can live to 16 years of age or longer. The life expectancy of a cat has doubled in the last 50 years.

Cats sleep about 16 hours a day. When awake they can run up to 30 miles per hour.

It is true, cats almost always land on their feet. This is because when dropped — even upside down — the cat will tuck in their front legs and extend its hind legs. This makes the back end of the cat have less rotation inertia. As a result, the cat's back end spins more than the front allowing the cat to always be in a position to land on all four paws.

Trivia

Easy
Why do cats have tails?
Answer: Cats use their tails for balance.

Challenging
Why does a cat purr?
Answer: Cats purr when they are happy, but also purr when they are distressed and/or in pain.

Bonus Round
In a household with two cats who gets along better — two cats of the same or opposite sex?
Answer: Cats of the opposite sex usually get along better.

Video

Understanding Cats — Produced by Roger Tabor — DVD, 2006.
Nature: Cats — Nature Archive Series, PBS — DVD, 1999.
The World of Cats Vols. 1 and 2 — Columbia River Entertainment — DVD, 2008.

Experiment: Is a cat left- or right-pawed?

Materials

- Cup of dry cat food
- Extra small paper cup (bathroom size)
- A friendly cat

Process
Place the cat food at the bottom of a cup too small for the cat to eat out of. Next, place the cup with cat food before the cat. Observe, which paw the cat uses? Try this before and after the video and/or with several different cats, one at a time.

Science behind the Experiment

Cats use whatever paw works best for the individual cat and/or for a specific task. They do not favor one paw over another.

Experiment References

Tripp, Geneva K. 2005. Are Cats Right-Pawed or Left-Pawed? California State Science Fair 2005 Project Summary. Retrieved August 7, 2010. www.usc.edu/cssf/history/2005.

Discussion

- Who owned a cat?
- Who are friendlier, dogs or cats?
- Which are smarter, dogs or cats?

Further Reading Suggestions

Mattern, Joanne. 2003. *The American Shorthair Cat.* Mankato, MN: Capstone High-Interest Books.
Neye, Emily with photos by Hathan, Elizabeth. 1999. *All about Cats and Kittens.* New York: Grosset & Dunlap.
Richards, James R. 1999. *The ASPCA Complete Guide to Cats.* San Francisco: Chronicle Books.

References

Cat Info. 2010. Cat Facts. Retrieved August 7, 2010. www.catsinfo.com/catfacts.html.
Freeman., Charles. 1997. *The Legacy of Ancient Egypt.* p. 17-65. New York: Facts on File, Inc.

Polar Bears

Introduction

The polar bear, the largest land carnivore, is born on land but spends most of its life on the sea ice. Scientists believe the polar bear diverged from the brown bear family when a group of bears became isolated in a glacier area about 200,000 years ago.

Home for a polar bear is the Arctic Circle and nearby land areas. They are a marine mammal because they prefer to live where the sea ice meets the Arctic waters where they hunt for seals, the main food of their diet.

An adult male polar bear weighs between 770 and 1,500 pounds and is about 7.9 to 9.8 feet in length. A female polar bear is half this size, but when pregnant can weigh about 1,100 pounds.

A polar bear has short stocky legs, small ears and tail, and very large feet with the pads of the paws covered by small, soft papillae resembling bumps. These bumps give the bear traction on ice. The bear's claws are deeply scooped to allow the bear to dig in ice.

In the hunt for food, mainly ringed and bearded seals, the polar bear uses its sense of smell, which can detect a seal about one mile away and under up to three feet of snow. The bear can see well at a distance and is equipped with 42 teeth.

Polar bears are excellent swimmers capable of traveling up to 200 miles from land at a rate of about six miles per hour. On land, the bear moves at about 3.5 miles per hour.

Trivia

Easy

What color is a polar bear?
Answer: White, however as the bear ages the coat yellows.

Challenging

Do polar bears hibernate?

Answer: No, polar bears are active year round. Female polar bears enter a den in the fall, give birth to cubs in November or December and remain in the den until March or April.

Bonus Round

How long do polar bear cubs remain with their mother?

Answer: Polar bear cubs at birth are blind and weigh about two pounds. They will nurse from their mother for about two and a half years as she teaches them to survive.

Video

The Wild Arctic — Topic Entertainment — DVD, 2008.
National Geographic's Polar Bear Alert — National Geographic Video — VHS, 1997.
Growing Up Arctic — Discovery, Gaiam — DVD, 2010.

Experiment: How do polar bears thrive in arctic waters?

Materials

- A 12-inch or larger diameter punchbowl, ¾ filled with cold water
- Two 12-inch square pieces of plastic food wrap
- Crisco or any shortening
- Scissors
- Hand towel

Process

Prior to the experiment:

Before the Science for Seniors program place a 1-inch layer of Crisco between the two pieces of plastic.

During the experiment:

At the program ask for a volunteer resident. Have the resident place his or her hand in the cold bowl of water. Remove and dry the hand.

Wrap the hand in the plastic Crisco sheets and return the resident's hand to the cold water. Ask the resident to describe the differences in the experience.

Science behind the Experiment

The shorting and plastic wrap simulates the 3.9-inch layer of blubber the polar bear has. Along with a dense hide and fur, the blubber layer protects the bear from extremely cold water and makes the polar bear a creature suited only for arctic climates. Polar bears could become extinct without an arctic climate; they would overheat in climates above 50 degrees.

Experiment References

Modified from:

Rita. 1999. Bear Science. Retrieved January 17, 2008.
   www.perpetualpreschool.com/preschool_themes/bears/bear_science.
   htm.

Discussion

- Who has seen a polar bear at the zoo?
- Has anyone seen a polar bear in the wild?
- Do you believe polar bears are in danger from global warming?

Further reading suggestions

Davids, Richard C. and photos by Guarvich, Dan. 1982. *Lords of the Arctic: A Journey among Polar Bears* New York: Macmillan.

Ellis, David. 2009. *On Thin Ice: The Changing World of the Polar Bear*. New York: Knopf.

Rosing, Norbert with Carney, Elizabeth. 2007. *Face to Face with Polar Bears*. Washington, DC: National Geographic.

References

National Geographic Kids. 2008. Polar Bears. National Geographic Society. Retrieved February 17, 2008.

http://kids.nationalgeographic.com/kids/animals/creaturefeature/
polar-bear/?vgnextfmt=printable.
Seaworld. 2002. Polar Bears. Retrieved February 17, 2008.
http://www.seaworld.org/infobooks/PolarBears/pbphysical.html.

Sharks

Introduction

There are over 350 species of sharks in the world with about 60 species living in the coastal North American waters. They range from the dogfish shark with a length of about 3.3 feet to the whale shark which can grow to about 50 feet in length.

Sharks are saltwater fish. A shark skeleton is made of cartilage and their body is covered with small scales. Sharks have lived in Earth's oceans for over 400 million years and in their current form for about 170 million years.

Large shark species have razor sharp teeth which are replaced continuously as teeth wear away. Known for eating other sea creatures, sharks have very keen senses that can even detect the breathing of a crab. However, sharks are not particular about their food. Scientists have discovered sharks eat dead fish and animals as well as human garbage including bottles, cans, and even tires.

Scientists are not sure why sharks attack humans. One theory is that sharks mistake humans for prey. A study of great white sharks found that from the bottom of the ocean a surfer can resemble a seal. Shark curiosity may be the reason some sharks bite a human and then swim away.

Trivia

Easy
What blockbuster movie was the story of a great white shark?
Answer: *Jaws.*

Challenging
How many species of sharks have attacked humans?
Answer: Thirty-five species have been reported in attacks on humans, but only about a dozen species attack on a regular basis.

Bonus Round

What was the largest great white shark found?
Answer: This shark was 20 feet, 4 inches long and weighed about 5,000 pounds.

Video

Shark Week: The 20ᵗʰ Anniversary (four discs) — Discovery Channel —
   DVD, 2005.
Shark Week: The Great Bites Collection (two discs) — Discovery
   Channel — DVD, 2009.
Shark Week: Ocean of Fear (two discs) — Discovery Channel — DVD,
   2008.

Experiment: How good is a shark's sense of smell?

Materials

- Three large drinking glasses
- Water
- Perfume or essential oils
- Marker
- Spoon
- Tape

Process

Prior to the experiment:

Prior to the Science for Seniors program label the glasses "A" for 10 drops, "B" for five drops and "C" for the glass with one drop. Fill the glasses with water and add the labeled amount of perfume. Stir the glasses.

During the experiment:

Ask the residents which glass has the strongest smell.

Science behind the Experiment

Sharks use their sense of smell to find food. A shark can smell the scent even if it is only 1/50 of a drop in a glass of water.

Experiment References

Singleton, Glen. 2007. *501 Science Experiments*. Experiment #161.
Heatherton, Australia: Hinkler Books Pty Ltd.

Discussion

- Who has seen a shark?
- Who has seen a movie about sharks?
- Did anyone ever live near a beach closed due to a shark sighting?

Further reading suggestions

Davies, Herbert David and Hobbs, Dorman. 1964. *About Sharks and Shark Attacks*. New York: Hobbs, Dorman.

Ellis, Richard. 1976. *The Book of Sharks*. New York: Grosset and Dunlap.

Peachin, Mary L. 2003. *The Complete Idiots Guide to Sharks*. Indianapolis: IN: Alpha Books.

References

Carnegie Library of Pittsburgh. 1997. *The Handy Science Answer Book*. Farmington Hills, MI: Visible Ink Press.

Fortey, Richard. 1998. *Life A Natural History of the First Four Billion Years of Life on Earth*. New York: Alfred A. Knopf.

Funk and Wagnalls, Inc. 1986. *New Encyclopedia of Science*. pp 1518-1519. Milwaukee, WI: Raintree Publishers Inc.

Sharks-world. 2010. Why Do Sharks Sometimes Attack? Retrieved August 20, 2010. http://www.sharks-world.com/why_do_sharks_sometimes_attack.html.

Creatures of the Forest

Introduction

There are more than one million animal species in the world. Most wild animals live in private lands and forests, state and national parks, or private and public zoos. Parks and zoos allow people to see wild animals that may naturally live in areas far away, and/or different climates and habitats.

Venezuela has the most national parks in the world. Over 22.2 percent of the land is devoted to the park system. Over 10 percent of United States lands are part of our national park system. The largest U.S. National Park is Wrangell-St. Elias in Alaska with 8,331,604 acres.

Zoos have collected, cared for, and displayed animals since about 1500 B.C. when the Egyptians established the first zoo. It was several hundred years later when Greek students studied animals and plants in zoo settings. Wealthy ancient Romans had private zoos.

When the Spanish arrived in Mexico in 1519, they discovered the Aztecs had zoos. The world's oldest existing zoo is Schonbrunn Zoo, established in 1752 in Austria.

The oldest zoo in the United States is Central Park Zoo in New York founded in 1854. This was followed by the Philadelphia Zoo in 1874, which is also home to the oldest children's zoo.

Trivia

Easy
What cartoon character is a forest creature that lives in the fictional Jellystone Park?
Answer: Yogi Bear.

Challenging

What creature was re-introduced to Yellowstone National Park despite rancher fears that the animal may kill cattle?

Answer: Wolves were re-introduced to the park in 1996. The National Park Service said tourists come from around the world to see wolves in the wild.

Bonus Round

What large brown creature was on the Yellowstone National Park threatened species list for 30 years, removed from the list in 2007, and returned to the endangered species list in 2009?

Answer: Grizzly bears. They were removed from the list in 2007 because their numbers had increased. They were placed back on the list in 2009 because of concerns of danger to the bears from global warming. The National Park Service monitors the numbers and habits of animals in the parks.

Video

Check with personnel at state and federal parks, the U.S. Fish and Wildlife Commission, the U.S. Department of Agriculture, local conservation organizations, and science museums. These sources may have available and be willing to loan and/or demonstrate science programs to the residents including films, slide shows, and animal pelts. I used a bag of pelts including bear, fox, rabbit, and squirrel that allowed the residents to feel the difference in the animal coats, coloring, and even teeth.

Jim Knox's Wild Safari at the San Diego Zoo's Wild Animal Park —
    Createspace — DVD, 2008.
Keepers of the Wild — National Geographic Society — DVD, 1993.
The Living Edens: Denali Alaska's Great Wilderness — PBS Home
    Video — DVD, 2005.

Experiment: Can you feel the difference between fox fur and rabbit fur?

If possible secure clean furs from the U.S. Fish and Wildlife Commission. This government agency loans materials for educational use. If this is not an option, try a taxidermy shop, a local museum, or ask friends, facility employees etc. for anyone willing to loan a rabbit and/or fox fur coat.

Materials

- Rabbit skin
- Fox skin
- Two cloth bags large enough to hold the furs

Process

Bring the furs into the program in separate cloth bags marked "A" and "B". Tell the residents to close their eyes. Walk around the room and let the residents feel both furs — rabbit (A) and fox (B). Then return to the front of the room. Hold up both furs and ask the residents to guess which was in bag A and which was in bag B.

Science behind the Experiment

Most humans are unaware of the different textures of animal skins and furs. This experiment shows the distinct adaptive nature of animal coats. Many mammals need fur to help regulate their body temperature. Different colors and textures serve the individual needs of the animal's home location and sometimes the color of the fur offers a way to hide from predators.

Experiment References

Created by Gloria Hoffner.

Discussion

- Who has seen a wild animal in a park?
- Who has visited a zoo?
- What is your favorite animal?

Further reading suggestions

Bradshaw, G. A. 2009. *Elephants on the Edge: What Animals Teach Us About Humanity*. New Haven: Yale University Press.

Harvard, Christian. 2005. *Untamed: Animals Around the World*. New York: H.N. Abrams.

Horton, Casey. 1988. *The Amazing Fact Book of Animals*. Mankato, MN: Creative Education.

References

Carnegie Library of Pittsburgh. 1997. *The Handy Science Answer Book*. Farmington Hills, MI.

Daniels, Donna. 2010. Grizzly Bears No Longer on the Threatened List around Yellowstone National Park. Retrieved August 20, 2010. http://www.associatedcontent.com/article/286646/grizzly_bears_no_longer_on_the_threatened.html?cat=16.

Funk and Wagnalls Inc. 1986. *Funk & Wagnalls New Encyclopedia of Science*. p. 1846. Milwaukee, WI: Raintree Publishers Inc.

Petiya, Scott. 2009. Yellowstone Grizzly Restored to Endangered Species List Overturning Bush Administration's Move. Retrieved August 20, 2010. http://www.associatedcontent.com/article/2227131/yellowstone_grizzly_restored_to_endangered.html?cat=47.

Welsch, Jeff. 2006. The First National Park is the Best Place to View Predators in the Wild: How to See Wolves in Yellowstone National Park. Retrieved August 20, 2010. http://www.associatedcontent.com/article/30013/how_to_see_wolves_in_yellowstone_national.html?cat=16.

Dinosaurs

Introduction

Dinosaurs lived on the Earth from about 250 to 65 million B.C. This is also the time of early fish, insects, and lizards. At the beginning of this period the Earth was one large continent called Pangaea.

Archeologists divide the time of the dinosaurs into periods. The first was the Triassic, which started about 250 million years ago and lasted about 50 million years. The phytosaur, taeniolabis, and palaeoryctes were a few of the dinosaur species to live during this period.

During the Triassic period, Earth's continents began to pull apart. Look at a map of Eastern North America and North Africa and you can see how at one time the continents would have fit together. The southern continents, what today we call Africa, South America, Australia, Antarctica, and India remained one joined mass called Gondwanaland.

Lasting from about 200 to 145 million years B.C. is the Jurassic period. The dinosaurs of this age included triceratops, brontosaurus, and pteranodon. Many of these dinosaurs lived mainly in the western United States and eastern Africa. It was also a time of further continental changes with Antarctica and Australia pulling away from Africa.

The Cretaceous period, from 145 million to about 65 million years B.C. brought flowering plants and trees. Dinosaurs, such as plesiosaurus, iguanodon, and gorgosaurus thrived in South America, India, and Australia as the continents settled into their current positions. This is the time of existence for the triceratops, tyrannosaurus, and lambeosaurus.

Dinosaurs died as a result of continental movements, planet temperature changes, diseases, etc. but scientists believe the final death blow to the dinosaurs was a meteor about six miles wide that hit the Earth 65 million years ago near the area we know as Cancun, Mexico. The impact threw massive amounts of dirt into the atmosphere blocking out the sun, resulting in the death of vegetation and food sources vital to the dinosaurs.

Trivia

Easy

What creature today is the descendant of dinosaurs?

Answer: Birds. This is based in part on the Archaeopteryx, a dinosaur similar in size to a chicken, which had feathers and could fly. It lived about 150 million years ago.

Challenging

What was the biggest dinosaur?

Answer: Argentinosaurus — A plant eater whose body was 120 feet from head to toe and weighed about 110 tons. This dinosaur lived 100 to 90 million years ago.

Bonus round

How many types of dinosaurs existed?

Answer: Scientists have evidence of about 440 different dinosaurs.

Video

Dinosaurs Alive — Image Entertainment — DVD, 2009.
When Dinosaurs Roamed America — Family Home Entertainment — DVD, 2001.
Chased by Dinosaurs — BBC Warner — DVD, 2004.

Experiment: How do fossils form?

Materials

- One cup coffee grounds
- ½ cup of cold coffee
- One cup of flour
- ½ cup of salt
- Quahog seashells and/or small rocks

Process
   Prior to the experiment:
   Prior to the Science for Seniors program, or allow an extra half hour to mix the ingredients with the residents, kneed the materials together. Place the mixture on paper plates and flatten on the plate.
   During the experiment:
   Next press some of the shells or rocks into the mixture. Leave some items pressed into the mixture until it hardens. With other material, such as the seashell, press the object firmly into the mixture and then remove it, making sure to leave the impression of the object in the mix on the plate. If possible make some of each so the residents can see the differences.
   After the experiment:
   Let harden for about two days.

Science behind the Experiment
   The items pressed into the mix as well as those removed show how fossils are formed from creatures and objects that make impressions in soft Earth or are trapped in soft earth. When the land hardens, the imprint or creature is preserved as a fossil. The objects that residents allowed to harden in the mix show that when dinosaurs and other creatures' bodies were trapped in the Earth their soft tissue decayed but the bones remained in the soil creating a fossil. The items removed are examples of dinosaurs walking in soft mud and the footprints creating a fossil.

Experiment References
Swanson, Marisa. 2010. Homemade Fossil Dough. Retrieved June 14,
      2010. www.ehow.com/way_5850416_homemade-fossil-dough-html.

Discussion

- Who has seen a dinosaur bone?
- Has anyone been to a site to dig for fossils?
- Did anyone want to be a paleontologist when they grew up?

Further reading suggestions

Bennett, Leonie. 2008. *Amazing Dinosaur Facts* New York: Bear Port Pub.
McNabb, Chris. 2009. *Complete Guide to Dinosaurs*. Edison, NJ: Book Sales Inc.
Norman, David. 1986. *The Age of the Dinosaurs*. New York: Bookwright Press.

References

Baker, Robert T. 1986. *The Dinosaur Heresies*. New York: Kensington Publishing Corp.
Busby III, Arthur B., Coenraads, Robert R., Willis, Paul and Roots, David. 1997. *The Nature Company Guide to Rocks and Fossils*. San Francisco: Time Life Books.
Fortey, Richard. 1998. *Life*. New York: Alfred A. Knopf, Inc.
Stout, William. 1981. *The Dinosaurs*. New York: Bantam Books Inc.
Swanson, Marisa. 2010. Homemade Fossil Dough. Retrieved June 14. www.ehow.com/way_58050416_homemade-fossil-dough.html.
Taquet, Philippe. 1998. *Dinosaur Impressions*. Cambridge: Cambridge University Press.
Watson, Jane Werner. 1981. *Dinosaurs and Other Prehistoric Reptiles*. New York: Golden Press.

Insects

Introduction

Insects arrived on Earth over 300 million years ago. The fossil records show that dragonflies have lived on Earth for over 250 million years and originally had a wingspan of over 28 inches.

There are 900 thousand known species of insects, but perhaps up to 30 million species when scientists include the probability of unknown species awaiting discovery in the rainforest and other remote locations.

In the U.S. there are about 91,000 species of insects, with perhaps another 73,000 living among us and yet uncategorized. There are several major categories: beetles, with about 23,700 species; flies with about 19,600 species; ants, bees, and wasps with about 17,500 species; and moths and butterflies with about 11,500 species.

While to most of us insects are annoying, they are a vital component in life on Earth because they are required for pollinating crops and flowers. About 130 crops in the United States are pollinated by bees representing a $9 billion value to farmers. One-third of the human diet, especially the diet of people living in developing nations, is connected to bee pollination.

Insects have been part of the human diet for more than 10,000 years. The Bible describes how John the Baptist thrived on locust and wild honey.

Insects, from termites to worms, remain a food source in Africa, Asia, and Latin America. Dragonflies, minus the wings, are boiled in coconut milk and served as a treat in Bali.

Trivia

Easy

True or false: A cockroach can live without his head.

Answer: True. How? Cockroaches do not have the huge blood supply or blood pressure that humans do. When they lose their head, they simply seal off that part of the body. They breathe through spiracles, tiny holes in each section of the body, which pump air directly to tissues. Cockroaches can survive weeks on a single meal. A well-fed headless cockroach will simply sit around breathing and living until eaten or until it dies of infection or starvation.

Challenging

What is the strongest insect on Earth?

Answer: The horn dung beetle can lift 1,141 times its weight. In human terms, that would equal a person capable of lifting six full double-decker buses or about 180,000 pounds.

Bonus round

What is the most dangerous insect in the world?

Answer: The jumping ant, the smallest of the red ants, can kill a person in four minutes by biting and injecting extremely poisonous venom. These bugs are found in Tasmania.

Video

Basic Facts about Insects — Educational Video Inc. — DVD, 2004.

Eyewitness: Insect — DK Publishing — DVD, 2007.

Natural History: Insects and Arachnids— A2ZCDS.Com, 2-DVD set, 2005.

Experiment: How do some insects walk on water?

Materials

- A clear 12-inch mixing bowl
- Water
- Paper clip
- Two-ounce bottle of dish soap

Process

Fill the bowl with water and gently place the paper clip on top of the surface of the water. See the paper clip sitting on top of the water. Now add a drop of dish soap to the water. The paper clip will sink.

Science behind the Experiment

The paper clip represents an insect such as a pond skimmer or a water strider. The insect stays on top of the water because of the water surface tension. Water surface tension happens when water molecules on the top and bottom of the water pull against each other causing something like a skin layer on the top of the water. The dish soap breaks up this layer causing the paper clip to fall into the water.

Experiment References

Home training tools. 2010. Water Experiments: Surface Tension Experiments. Retrieved June 17, 2010. www.hometrainingtools.com/water-experiments/a/1272/

Discussion

- Who has eaten a bug?
- Who had an ant colony as a child?
- Did anyone keep bees or know a beekeeper?

Further reading suggestions

Chinery, Michael. 2008. *Amazing Insects: Images of Fascinating Creatures.* Richmond Hill, ON: Firefly Books.
Parker, Steve. 2005. *Ant Lions, Wasps, and Other Insects.* Minneapolis: Compass Point Books.

Llewelyn, Claire and illustrated by Forsey, Christopher, Riccardi, Andrea
  and Wright, David. 2005. *The Best Book of Bugs*. Oakland, CA:
  Kingfish.

References

caes.uga.edu. 2010. Pollination: Economic Impact. Retrieved August 20,
  2010. http://interests.caes.uga.edu/insectlab/agimpact.html.
Carnegie Library of Pittsburgh. 1997. *The Handy Science Answer Book*.
  Detroit, MI: Visible Ink Press.
holoweb. 2010. Dragonflies. Retrieved August 20, 2010.
  http://www.holoweb.com/cannon/dragonfl.htm.

Chapter 3 — Ecology

In this day and age we hear many theories of how our earth is changing due to human actions. Some of these theories include global warming, acid rain, and different types of pollution. This chapter is dedicated to exploring these topics and discussing how and why they happen, and what we can do to help combat the problems that arise from humans being on the planet. This chapter also will take you to a world most of us have never seen — the rainforest. From this chapter your knowledge of ecology will flourish.

Global Warming

Introduction

What is global warming? Global warming, according to the U.S. Environmental Protection Agency, refers to the increase in the Earth's average temperature. A change in temperature can lead to climate change including more or less rainfall affecting crop growth, animals, and food supply. Rising temperatures could also cause melting ice caps, which could raise sea levels and impact coastal cities.

Scientists know the Earth's temperature has increased by almost one degree in the past century. It is expected to rise another two to six degrees over the next century. What may sound like a very small level of change could have very big consequences for the Earth's population. During the last ice age, about 18,000 years ago, the Earth was only seven degrees colder than today and yet that was a time when glaciers covered most of North America.

What causes global warming? There are several causes including changes in the sun's intensity, changes in ocean circulation, and human behavior. Many scientists are concerned that human behavior during the last 200 years, burning of fossil fuel, building urban centers, and fast-paced deforestation, has increased pollution in the Earth's atmosphere therefore trapping heat and artificially warming the planet. This was strongly supported by a 2012 NASA study that compared the amount of solar energy absorbed by the Earth's surface to the amount returned to space as heat from 2005 to 2010. The result was that during this period, despite unusually low solar activity, the Earth retained more heat than it returned to space. "This provides unequivocal evidence that the sun is not the dominant driver of global warming," said James Hansen, director of NASA's Goddard Institute for Space Studies, who led the research.

What changes can occur as a result of global warming? The National Geographic Society reports:

- The Arctic could see an ice-free summer in 2040 or earlier.

- Polar bears and other Arctic creatures have to travel farther for food as a result of the loss of sea ice.
- Glaciers and mountain snows are melting. Montana's Glacier National Park has 27 glaciers — there were 150 glaciers in the park in 1910.
- Some scientists believe the increase in wildfires, heat waves, and strong tropical storms is due to climate change.

There are scientists who do not believe in global warming. Khabibullo Abdusamatov, a chief researcher at the Russian Academy of Sciences, made a 2006 report stating he believed temperatures would drop from 2012 to 2015 and would continue to drop for about 60 years.

In 1971, S.I. Rasool and S.H. Schneider at the Institute for Space Studies published a paper saying growing aerosol levels in the atmosphere would bring about a new ice age. However, the aerosol levels in the atmosphere actually decreased since their publication, which invalidated their theory.

Trivia

Easy
Name one American state where you can find a glacier?
Answer: Alaska, Montana, Washington, California, Colorado, Wyoming, Oregon, Nevada, Idaho, and Utah.

Challenging
What would happen if all the ice sheets including the polar ice caps and all glaciers on Earth melted?
Answer: The sea level worldwide would rise about 250 feet flooding coastal cities and affecting over 150 million people worldwide.

Bonus Round
What mountain in Africa has lost 40 percent of its ice in the last 25 years?
Answer: Mt. Kenya's Lewis Glacier in East Africa has lost 40 percent of its ice in 25 years.

Video

Global Warming: The Signs and the Science — PBS Home Video —
    DVD, 2006.
National Geographic: Six Degrees Could Change the World — National
    Geographic Video — DVD, 2008.
NOVA: Global Warming: What's up with the Weather — PBS NOVA —
    DVD, 2007.

Experiment: How would global warming change coastlines around the world?

Materials

- Warming tray
- Large punch bowl, minimum width 12 inches
- Cold water
- 10-inch plastic container
- Ice frozen into the rough shape of an iceberg
- Blue masking tape

If possible, place the warming tray and the punch bowl on a moving cart so the demonstration can be brought close to residents with low vision.

Process

Prior to the experiment:

Prior to the Science for Seniors program fill the 10-inch plastic container with water and freeze.

During the experiment:

At the beginning of the program, place the punchbowl on the warming tray. Fill the punchbowl with warm water and place the ice (stand-in for an iceberg) in the punchbowl so it floats. Place a ring of masking tape around the outside of the punchbowl to mark the top of the water level in the bowl prior to global warming. Turn on the warming tray.

Science behind the Experiment

The punchbowl represents the Earth. The water is the Earth's seas and oceans. The line of blue tape represents coastlines around the planet. The mini-iceberg represents the existing arctic ice floes. As the residents watch the global warming video, the warming tray will heat up the water in the bowl just as global warming heats the Earth's oceans. When the film is over, point out that, as the iceberg melted, the water rose in the bowl over the line of blue tape. This demonstrates that if the Earth's arctic ice melts, rising ocean waters would flood coastal cities.

Experiment References

Created by Gloria Hoffner.

Discussion

- Who has seen a glacier?
- Do you believe the climate is changing?
- What do you think should be done?

Further reading suggestions

Houghton, John. 2009. *Global Warming: The Complete Briefing*. New York: Cambridge University Press.

Long, Douglass. 2003. *Global Warming*. New York: Facts on File.

Rosser, Simon and Billington, Russ. 2008. *A-Z of Global Warming*. New York: Schmall World Publishing.

References

Hile, Kevin. 2009. *The Handy Weather Answer Book*. Detroit, MI: Visible Ink Press.

Koch, Wendy, 2012. NASA: Global warming caused mostly by humans. *USA TODAY*, Jan 31, 2012.
http://content.usatoday.com/communities/greenhouse/post/2012/01/nasa-global-warming-caused-mostly-by-humans/1

National Geographic. 2007. Global Warming Fast Facts. Retrieved May 9, 2009. http://news.nationalgeographic.com/news/2004/12/1206_041206_global_warming.html.

Acid Rain

Introduction

Acid rain is a combination of wet and dry materials in the atmosphere with higher than normal levels of nitric and sulfuric acids. It forms in the atmosphere as a result of natural causes such as plant decay and volcanic eruptions or by man-made causes such as the burning coal.

When nitric and sulfuric acids enter the air during wet conditions, including fog and snow, the acid will return to the Earth in the rain, snow, fog, or mist. In dry conditions, the acid enters the atmosphere and can be blown great distances and can stick to the ground.

The dilemma of acid rain was discovered in the 1960s when great numbers of fish were dying in Scandinavian lakes. Looking for answers, researchers discovered acid from European industries was mixing in the atmosphere and creating acid snow and rain. This resulted in lake water becoming so acidic that it killed the fish.

The Great Smokey Mountains National Park, which has been inhabited by humans for more than 11,000 years, is showing damage from acid rain. Located between Tennessee and North Carolina, the 814 square mile forest became a national park in 1934.

This area is called the Smokey Mountains because in the early morning the mists rising from the trees resemble smoke from a cabin chimney. The National Park Service reports that the average pH of the rainfall in the park is 4.5, which is five to ten times more acidic than normal rainfall. This rain has resulted in the death of hardwood trees located at the top of the Smokey Mountains.

The National Park Service believes the acid rain, which is killing the trees, is created by the combination of automobile exhaust and air pollution from coal burning power plants. When the pollution mixes with the high rainfall experienced in the Smokey Mountains, it results in poisoned soil.

Trivia

Easy
Do cars contribute to acid rain?
Answer: Yes. Car exhausts contain nitrogen oxide.

Challenging
How much sulfur and nitrogen oxides does the United States discharge into the atmosphere?
Answer: About 40 metric tons each year.

Bonus Round
What area of the United States has the highest concentration of acid rain?
Answer: The highest acid rain levels are in Lake Erie and Lake Ontario.

Video

Acid Rain — Educational Video Network — DVD, 2004.
Acid Rain: New Bad News — NOVA on PBS — VHS.
Planet in Peril — CNN, Warner Home Video — two DVDs (contains information about acid rain, as well as other threats to the ecology of the planet), 2008.

Experiment: What is the effect of acid rain on plants?

Materials

- Three jars with lids
- Three growing bean plants in small cups or small, separate planting containers
- Masking tape
- Marking pen
- Lemon juice
- Water
- Tablespoon

Process

Grow three seed plants in paper cups and mark the cups A, B, and C. The experiment will work best if you first allow the plants to reach a height of six inches. Fill three jars as follows:

A — ½ cup of lemon juice and ½ cup of water;

B — ¼ cup lemon juice and ¾ cup water and

C — all water.

After the plants have grown to about six inches, water the plants with four tablespoons of liquid from their matching jar each day.

Science behind the Experiment

The lemon juice and lemon and water mix simulate acid rain. Plant A will first show the signs of acidic watering including shriveled leaves. Plant B, receiving lesser strength acidic watering, will take longer to look like plant A. Plant C will show no effects since it is receiving non-acidic water. The three plants show the effect of acid rain on plant life.

Experiment References

Weird Science Kids. 2010. Retrieved June 17, 2010.
    http://weirdsciencekids.com/AcidRainExperiment.html.

Discussion

- Who has been to the Smokey Mountains?
- Who has worked in a factory powered by coal?
- What do you think should be done about acid rain?

Further reading suggestions

Allaby, Michael, illustrations by Garratt, Richard. 2003. *Fog, Smog and Poison Rain*. New York: Facts on File.

Ostmann Jr., Robert. 1982. *Acid Rain: A Plague Upon the Waters* Minneapolis, MN: Dillon Press.

Tyson, Peter. 1992. *Acid Rain*. New York: Chelsea House.

References

Appalachian Voice Staff. 2001. Survey: Northern Hardwoods Dying in West Virginia, Pennsylvania. Retrieved August 16, 2010. http://membrane.com/trees/ozone.html.

OH ranger. 2010. Smokey Mountains. Retrieved July 16, 2010. http://www.ohranger.com/smoky-mountains/toc/history-culture.

U.S. EPA. 2010. What is Acid Rain? Retrieved July 16, 2010. www.epa.gov/acidrain/what/.

Air Pollution

Introduction

As long as there has been a planet Earth, there has been air pollution. In the past air pollution was caused by smoke, volcanic ash, dust, and pollens. These still exist, but modern humans have added a new form of pollution to the planet: chemical and industrial particles.

In 2002 United States automobile usage resulted in 346 tons of carbon monoxide each day. However, America is not alone in creating pollution. Some of the most polluted air in the world can be found in Cairo, Egypt, Shenyang, China, and Delhi, India. The problem increases each day as more and more people around the world exchange other forms of travel such as walking or biking for cars.

It is not just the automobiles. In the United States alone at every moment there are more than 5,000 airplanes in the sky. The planes burn fuels that contribute nitrogen oxides, sulfur dioxide, and carbon monoxide to the air.

Scientists estimate millions of dollars is lost each year due to crops that fail to grow because of air pollution.

A 2010 report by the National Parks Conservation Association found that air pollution from cities and power plants hundreds of miles away was polluting the air at the Grand Canyon National Park. The Environmental Protection Agency is considering stronger emissions laws on power plants to help clear the pollution at the Grand Canyon National Park.

Trivia

Easy
Does air pollution reach the North Pole?
Answer: Yes. Winds carry pollution around the globe.

Challenging

What is a smog alert?

Answer: The government issues a smog alert when air conditions may lead to respiratory problems for people with health conditions such as asthma.

Bonus Round

What is a major source of air pollution that is not related to transportation?

Answer: Burning fossil fuels, coal and oil, for generating heat and electricity. The United States has worked to reduce these emissions but they remain a serious concern in developing countries.

Video

Air Pollution, Smog, and Acid Rain — Educational Video Network, Inc.
  — DVD, 2004.
What Price Clean Air — Richter Productions — DVD, 2009.
American Experience: Earth Days — PBS — DVD, 2010.

Experiment: Can you see air pollution?

Materials

- Six feet of cheesecloth
- Masking tape
- Telephone pole or tree in high traffic parking lot
- Telephone pole or tree located in park or forest
- Telephone pole or tree near your facility

Process

Prior to the experiment:

Wrap cheesecloth around a tree or telephone pole in a high traffic area and attached with masking tape. Do the same with the tree in a park or forest and in the location near your facility. Leave up for two months.

During the experiment:

Take down and compare. Discuss whether your facility is more like a park or more like a high traffic area.

Science behind the Experiment

The cloth in the high traffic areas will show the carbon particles from car exhaust while the cloth placed in the park will show fewer particles. This demonstrates the pollution caused by automobile engines.

Experiment References

Created by Richard Hoffner-McCall, author's son, for school and Eagle
  Scout project in 2000.

Discussion

- What do you think should be done about air pollution?
- Did you ever attend Earth Day events?
- Has your health been affected by air quality?

Further reading suggestions

Dhillon, Sukharai S. 1987. *Industrial Leaks and Air Pollution: Causes,
  Cures and Health Concerns*. Dayton, OH: Pamphlet Publications.
Seinfeld, John H. and Pandis, Spyros N. 2006. *Atmospheric Chemistry
  and Physics from Air Pollution to Climate Change. 2nd edition*
  Hoboken, NJ: Wiley-Interscience.
Vallero, Daniel A. 2007. *Fundamentals of Air Pollution*. Maryland
  Heights, MO: Academic Press.

References

CNN. 1998. Air Pollution Additive Contaminating California Water.
  Retrieved August 16, 2010. http://articles.cnn.com/1998-06-
  03/tech/9806_03_california.water_1_mtbe-contamination-drinking-
  water-water-agencies?_s=PM:TECH.
McKinnon, Shaun. 2010. Grand Canyon's Future at Grave Risk.
  Retrieved August 16, 2010.
  http://www.azcentral.com/news/articles/2010/08/24/20100824grand-
  canyon-future-at-risk.html.

Light Pollution

Introduction

Less than one-fifth of the world's population, most of who are living in England, Europe, and the United States, have seen the Milky Way, our home galaxy, against the night sky. In the United States, less than two-thirds of the residents can view the Milky Way from their hometowns.

This is due to light pollution. Light pollution is caused by artificial light that interferes with astronomical observation. Some scientists believe the overuse and misdirection of nighttime lighting is confusing to birds, dangerous for insects killed by flying too close to the light, and may also affect human sleep patterns.

Light pollution is costly. David Crawford, an astronomer, has estimated the United States spends about two billion dollars a year on wasted lighting. A few states, such as Maine, Arizona, New Mexico, Texas, and Connecticut have passed laws to control and limit light pollution.

The solution is not turning off all outdoor lighting, but rather using appropriate lighting and directing it downward. Astronomers suggest lower pressure sodium lighting with shielded bulbs to direct lighting where needed and not upward into the sky.

Trivia

Easy

What star is commonly used as a navigational reference?

Answer: Polaris, which is commonly known as the North Star.

Challenging

Who chooses a name for a new star, planet or comet discovery?

Answer: The International Astronomical Union is a professional organization that helps those who discover a new space body to create an appropriate name. Private companies who offer to "name a star after a loved one" for fees have no legal standing.

Bonus Round

What is one of the oldest star gazing locations on Earth?

Answer: Stonehenge, a circle of stones located in England, was built between 2500 and 1700 B.C. Archeologists believe it was constructed to observe the midsummer and midwinter solstices.

Video

400 Years of the Telescope — PBS Direct — DVD, 2009.

Needless Light Pollution — this is a series of eight free, light pollution videos available on the website: www.need-less.org.uk/animations.php.

Earth Observatory: Image of the Day — NASA — this website will allow you to show residents a map of the globe showing where most light pollution occurs — http://earthobservatory.NASA.gov/IOTD.

Experiment: What is light pollution?

Materials

- Glow in the dark stars (available in toy and craft shops)
- Dark room
- Flashlights
- Tape

Process

Prior to the experiment:

Prior to the Science for Seniors program, stick a large number of glow in the dark stars to the ceiling of the room you are using. If possible, use a small windowless room to eliminate as much light as you can. To avoid problems with the stick-on stars remaining on the ceiling, attach the stars with tape for easy removal.

Put the lights on in the room about two hours before the program to make sure the stars have time to absorb light.

During the experiment:

At the start of the program, bring the residents into the room. Give each resident a turned-off flashlight. Once everyone is seated, turn off all light in the room. Allow the residents time to take in the star-filled ceiling as if they were outdoors at night.

Next have residents turn on their flashlights taking turns adding light to the room one by one.

Science behind the Experiment

As the residents turn on the flashlights, this light will wash out the glow from the artificial stars. This simulates how artificial lighting, such as city streetlights, parking lot lights, store signs, etc. dims the view of the stars in the night sky.

Experiment References

Created by Gloria Hoffner.

Discussion

- How many have seen the Milky Way?
- Do you notice fewer stars in the sky now than you remember viewing as a child?
- Do you think your grandchildren see more or less stars from their backyards?

Further reading suggestions

Boger, Paul. 2008. *Let There Be Night: Testimony on Behalf of the Dark*. Reno, NV: University of Nevada Press.

Crelin, Bob and Ziner, Annie. 2007. *There Once Was a Sky Full of Stars*. Cambridge, MA: Sky Publishing.

Mizon, Bob. 2001. *Light Pollution: Responses and Remedies*. New York: Springer.

References

Catchpole, Heather. 2009. One-fifth of Us Have Lost Sight of the Milky Way. Retrieved August 16, 2010. http://www.cosmosmagazine.com/news/2797/one-fifth-us-have-lost-sight-milky-way?page=1.

Darling, David. 2004. *The Universal Book of Astronomy: From the Andromeda Galaxy to the Zone of Avoidance*. Hoboken, NJ: John Wiley and Sons, Inc.

Levy, David H. 1994. *The Nature Company Guides Skywatching*. San Francisco: Time Life Books.

Quandt, Matt. 2010. *The Dark Night Goes Quietly*. Retrieved August 16, 2010. www.astronomy.com/asy/default.aspx?c=a7id-=2249.

Tyson, Neil de Grasse. 2004. *The Sky Is Not The Limit: Adventures of an Urban Astrophysicist*. Amherst, NY: Prometheus Books.

Space Pollution

Introduction

Ever since the launch of Sputnik in 1957, humankind has been filling the space surroun ing the Earth with artificial creations. NASA estimates there are about 3,000 in-use satellites orbiting the Earth, plus another 6,000 out-of-use satellites. These numbers do not include rocket boosters and other space junk floating around the planet. In June of 2010 NASA estimated there were about 13,000 objects larger than a softball, 100,000 larger than a penny, and tens of millions of smaller objects.

Out of site for most humans, these orbiting pieces of junk can present a real threat to the safety of astronauts and sometimes for people living on Earth.

The Skylab Space Station was built by the United States and orbited the Earth from 1973 to 1979. It was 118 feet long, 21 feet in diameter, and weighed about 100 tons. When it fell into a lower orbit earlier than expected, NASA could not send a crew to the station in time to stabilize the craft. It fell to Earth on July 11, 1979, scattering pieces across the Indian Ocean and on land in western Australia. No one was injured.

In 2009, the Space Shuttle Discovery was forced to dodge a piece of a Chinese satellite and had two other near misses of space junk. Orbiting as fast as 18,000 miles per hour most seven times faster than a bullet, a piece of space junk the size of a bowling ball could hit the space station with an impa t of 300 miles per hour.

Trivia

Easy

Earth is ringed by satellites and space junk. Which planets in our solar system have natural rings?
Answer: Jupiter, Saturn, Uranus, and Neptune all have rings. Rings are made of small particles of ice as well as large pieces of asteroids left over from the time of the creation of the solar system.

Challenging

How do astronauts protect themselves in space?
Answer: The International Space Station is equipped with rockets to move it out of the way of space junk. The shuttle is equipped with shields to protect it from the impact of small debris.

Bonus Round

What happens when space debris loses its orbit around the Earth?
Answer: Since most of the Earth's surface is water, large space junk usually lands in the oceans. Smaller debris usually burns up as it re-enters the Earth's atmosphere.

Video

NASA Skylab Missions, Challenges and Successes — The Historical Archives — DVD.
NASA Space Trek Vol. 4: Skylab the Second Manned Mission — FastForward, Pinnacle Vision — DVD.
Space Stations — A & E Home Video — DVD, 2006.

Experiment: How do objects appear when they burn up entering Earth's atmosphere?

Materials

- Alka-Seltzer tablets
- Clear vase
- Water

Process

Have residents watch the water as a volunteer resident tosses the tablet into the vase. The fizzing represents an object burning up as it enters Earth's atmosphere.

Science behind the Experiment

As an object enters the Earth's atmosphere the air in front of the object is compressed and heats up. This heat burns up the object. Space shuttles are covered with heat shields to protect the craft during re-entry.

Experiment References

Created by Gloria Hoffner.

Discussion

* Who remembers Skylab?
* In the summer of 1979, did you worry about Skylab falling into an inhabited area?
* Who would like or would have liked to live on a space station?

Further Reading Suggestions

Asimov, Isaac. 2006. *Space Junk*. Milwaukee, WI: Gareth Stevens Pub.
Belew, Leland F., editor and prepared by the George C. Marshall Flight Center. 1997. *Skylab: Our First Space Station*. Washington DC: National Aeronautics and Space Administration.
Hitt, David, Garriott, Owen, and Kerwin, Joe. 2008. *Homesteading Space: The Skylab Story*. Lincoln, NE: University of Nebraska Press.

References

Engelbert, Phillis and Dupuis, Diane L. 1998. *The Handy Space Answer Book*. Detroit, MI: Visible Ink Press.
NASA.gov. 2010. What is Orbital Debris? Retrieved August 16, 2010. www.NASA.gov/audience/forstudents/k-4/stories/what-is-orbital-debris-k4.html.

Planetary.org. 2008. Planetary News: Asteroids and Comets. Retrieved January 28, 2010. http://planetary.org/news/2008/1006_BoulderSized_Asteroid_will_Burn_Up_in.html.

Rinard, Judith A. 2007. *The Story of Flight.* Toronto, Canada: Firefly Books.

Space.com. 2009. Space Junk Problem Detailed. Retrieved August 16, 2010. www.space.com/news/0900912-space-junk-images.html.

Rainforests

Introduction

A rainforest is defined as any dense vegetation area that receives over 40 inches of rain a year. The Earth's rainforests once covered about 14 percent of the Earth's surface. Due to logging, farming, and other uses for the land, rainforest now make up only about six percent of the Earth.

The Amazon Rainforest covers a billion acres and has been called the Lungs of the Earth. This is because more than 20 percent of the world's oxygen is produced when the plants of the rainforest convert carbon dioxide into oxygen.

Flowing more than 4,000 miles from the Andes Mountains to the Atlantic Ocean, the Amazon River is the largest river system in the world. It is fed by over 1,100 tributaries and in sections is over 300 miles wide. More than two thirds of the world's fresh water is located in the Amazon Basin.

This area has the largest collection of plant and animal species in the world. In the rainforest an areas as small as 2½ acres can include over 750 trees and 1,500 other plants.

There are over 3,000 kinds of fruit in the rainforest. About 200 of these are used in the Western world. Pharmaceutical companies have developed about 120 prescription drugs from plants, about 25 percent of them come from rainforest ingredients. Less than one percent of rainforest trees and plants have been tested for medical purposes.

Trivia

Easy

Name a country containing a part of the Amazon Rainforest.
Answer: Brazil, Venezuela, Colombia, Ecuador, and Peru.

Challenging

Name a food that comes from the rainforest.

Answer: Avocados, coconuts, figs, oranges, lemons, grapefruit, bananas, pineapples, mangos, tomatoes, corn, potatoes, and rice.

Bonus round

There were 10 million indigenous tribal members living in the Amazon rainforest five centuries ago. How many people live in the rainforest today?

Answer: Less than 200,000.

Video

Classic Rainforest— National Geographic — DVD, 1993.

The Rainforest — Schlessinger Video Productions a division of Library Video Company — VHS, 1993.

IMAX Presents Tropical Rainforests — Vista Point Entertainment — DVD, 2005 (this is a Danish film with English subtitles)

Experiment: How do the rainforest spiders keep from sticking to their own webs?

Materials

- Masking tape
- Vegetable oil
- Paper cup
- Paper towel
- Volunteers

Process

Fill a cup halfway full with vegetable oil. Wrap a band of masking tape — sticky side up — around the volunteer's right hand. Ask the volunteer to place a finger from their left hand on the sticky masking tape to feel how the finger sticks to the tape.

Next ask the volunteer to place a finger in the cup with vegetable oil. Now ask the volunteer to place the oily finger on the sticky tape. The finger will not stick when covered with oil.

Science behind the Experiment

The sticky tape represents the spider web that traps and holds the spider's victims. The vegetable oil represents substances on the feet of the spider that allows the spider to move easily over the web without becoming stuck.

Experiment References

Tree frog treks. 2010. Ask Mr. Science: Spider Webs. Retrieved August 18, 2010. www.treefrogtreks.com/blog/?p=1338.

Discussion

- Have you ever visited a rainforest?
- What do you think should be done to save the rainforests?
- Would you pay a tax on rainforest foods to help save the rainforests?

Further reading suggestions

Caufield, Catherine. 1986. *In the Rainforest*. Chicago, IL: University of Chicago Press.
Cothran, Helen. 2003. *Global Resources/Opposing Viewpoints*. San Diego, CA: Greenhaven Press.
Reader's Digest Association, 2002. *Mysteries of the Rainforest*. London, England: Readers Digest Books.

References

Raintree.com. 2008. Rainforest Facts. The Disappearing Rainforests. Retrieved July 3, 2008. http://rain-tree.com/facts.htm
Tucci, Paul A. and Rosenberg, Matthew T. 2009. *The Handy Geography Answer Book*. Detroit, MI: Visible Ink Press.

Water Pollution

Introduction

Water is necessary for all life on Earth. Some the water on the planet is original to the planet's earliest days, but water is still being added when comets and other space objects containing water hit the Earth. The water you drink has existed for billions of years in a liquid, solid, or gaseous state.

Ninety-seven percent of the Earth's water is salt water which in its natural state cannot be used for drinking or irrigation. About two percent of the planet's water is frozen in glaciers and ice sheets. That gives the world only about .8 percent for human and animal consumption.

In the average American home water usage averages are 41 percent for flushing toilets, 37 percent for bathing, and 22 percent for washing dishes, clothing, cooking, drinking, cleaning, and gardening. Other large users of water in the country include industry, agriculture, and thermoelectric power.

Water pollution can happen by natural causes such as volcanic ash or artificial causes including oil, fertilizer, pesticides, and households dumping unused prescription medications down the drain. In 2002, the U.S. Geological Survey found prescription chemicals in 80 percent of American streams.

Freshwater pollution in the United States has resulted in 40 percent of America's rivers and 46 percent of the lakes being too polluted for fishing or swimming. In addition, 1.2 trillion gallons of untreated sewerage, storm water, and industrial waste flow into U.S.'s fresh waters each year.

Oceans cover 70% of the Earth's surface. Oceans become polluted when trash and other materials are dumped from private and commercial ships, discharged from factories, and allowed to run off from crop and animal farms. Scientists have reported damage to the oxygen producing creatures, fish populations, and coral reefs due to ocean pollution.

Plastic bags, aluminum cans, and other items improperly disposed of by humans create a threat to ocean life. Sea turtles can mistake plastic shopping bags for sea jellies, a source of food for the sea turtle. If a turtle eats a plastic bag, the turtle will choke and die.

Aluminum cans have been found in the deepest oceans. In 1950, U.S. Admiral R. J. Galanson discovered a beer can seven miles down on the floor of the Pacific Ocean.

Trivia

Easy
How much fresh water is used in farming?
Answer: About 60 percent of the world's water is used in irrigation. This equals about 137 billion gallons per day.

Challenging
Do dams affect the planet's water cycle?
Answer: Yes. Dams change fresh water flow and can affect the temperature and cloud formation in the area due to the artificial creation of a large body of water.

Bonus Round
What was the London Great Smog?
Answer: In 1952 the high level of sulfur dioxide in the air created an acid fog so dense people could not see through it. It resulted in sickening about 100,000 people and caused about 4,000 deaths among people suffering from influenza, bronchitis, and pneumonia.

Video

The Blue Planet: Seas of Life — a BBC/Discovery Co-Production — set of five DVDs.
Eyewitness Ocean — DK Vision and BBC Worldwide Americas — DVD.
Ocean Drifters — National Geographic Society — VHS.

Experiment: What is a natural way to clean up an oil spill in the ocean?

Materials

- Clear 10" x 13" baking pan
- Water
- Motor oil
- Clean cut human hair
- Pencil or similar sized stick

Process

Place the water in the pan about ¾ full. Pour a layer of oil on the surface of the water. Place the human hair on the oil and push the hair into the oil with the pencil/stick. Push the oily hair to the side of the pan. The water without hair will be clear.

Science behind the Experiment

Human hair absorbs oil. This method was used with some success for clean up during the BP Gulf Oil Spill in 2010. This method of cleaning was limited due to the limited amount of hair available.

The oil well that was creating the spill was capped August 16, 2010, according to CNN.com. On August 24, 2010, CBSnews.com reported scientists studying the oil spill discovered a new microbe that was eating the oil without significantly depleting oxygen in the water.

Experiment References

After seeing a news report on CNN's "American Morning" that human hair might be a way to soak up the oil from the spill, Gloria Hoffner devised this experiment to try with the residents at Sterling Healthcare and Rehabilitation in Media, PA.

Discussion

- Have you ever been affected by an oil spill or other type of water pollution?
- What are the roles of government and industry in making sure there is enough clean water for everyone?

- What can individuals do to prevent water pollution?

Further reading suggestions

Aylesworth, Thomas G. 1973. *This Vital Air, This Vital Water: Man's Environmental Crisis.* Skokie, IL: Rand McNally.

Clarke, Robin and King, Janet. 2009. *The Atlas of Water.* Berkeley: University of California Press.

Dolan, Edward F. 1997. *Our Poisoned Waters.* New York: Dutton.

References

AARP Bulletin. 2007. Before You Pour It Down the Drain. Vol.48. No. 1.

Grinning Planet. 2005. Atomic Cannonball off the High Dive and Other Causes of Water Pollution. Retrieved August 16, 2010. http://www.grinningplanet.com/2005/09-06/water-pollution-causes-article.htm.

Hazen, Terry. 2010. Deepwater Plume Does Not Significantly Deplete Oxygen in Water as It Consumes Oil. Retrieved August 14, 2010. http://www.cbsnews.com/stories/2010/08/24/tech/main6801526.shtml?tag=contentMain;contentBody.

Hile, Kevin. 2009. *The Handy Weather Answer Book.* Canton, MI: Visible Ink Press.

Nye, Bill. 1999. *The Great Big Book of Science.* New York: Hyperion Paperbacks for Children.

Science News. 2011. First Comet Found With Ocean-Like Water. Retrieved January 26, 2012. http://www.sciencedaily.com/releases/2011/10/111005131654.htm

Tucci, Paul A. and Rosenberg, Matthew T. 2009. *The Handy Geography Answer Book.* Detroit, MI: Visible Ink Press.

U.S. Geological Survey. 2008. *Groundwater Atlas of the United States.* Available on line and through the U.S. Government Services.

Chapter 4 — Energy

Humans have always used energy, from the earliest forms of energy use when humans used the sun to cook and dry food to the use of coal for heat and cooking. As time progressed our abilities to utilize different forms of energy also progressed. We created steam engines and harnessed power from the wind, water, and sun. This chapter will give you a number of engaging experiments to show you how humans accomplished these feats.

Electricity

Introduction

Electricity is produced when electrons move through the atoms of matter. In an electrical wire or cord, electrons pass from one atom to the next creating a steady electrical current.

Electricity flows best when the electrons are loosely held. Materials that are good conductors of electricity include copper, aluminum, and steel. Substances that are poor conductors of electricity are called insulators. Rubber, cloth, plastic, and glass are examples of insulators.

Electricity is used in our homes to power the television, the computer, to turn on and off heating and cooling systems, and of course for the electric light.

Benjamin Franklin is famous for flying a kite with a key attached to the kite tail during a lightning storm in June of 1752. He had conducted electrical experiments from the early 1700s and was convinced of a connection between electricity and lightning. He stood on the steeple of Christ Church in Philadelphia with a kite, a key attached to the kite, and a ribbon wrapped around his hand as insulation. At the first sign of an electric charge hitting the key, Franklin dropped the kite. Historians think he was not injured because he did the experiment when the storm was weak and because he was very lucky!

A few years before the kite experiment, in 1749, Franklin had an idea for an electric battery. However, he could not think of a use for the battery, the same electric storage device we use to power many things from cars to watches.

Trivia

Easy
What forms of energy are used to make electricity?
Answer: Coal, steam, solar, natural gas, geothermal, wind, and water.

Challenging

Why can birds sit on an electric wire without harm?

Answer: The birds and any other creatures including humans are safe as long as they touch only one wire and are not grounded. Touching both wires at the same time or touching the ground and a charged high-voltage wire would result in electrocution.

Bonus Round

Who created the electric light bulb?

Answer: Sir Humphrey Davy created the first light by passing electricity through a thin platinum wire. Thomas Edison in 1878 created a light bulb that was cool enough to be used in a home.

Video

Heat — Frontline co-production with RAINMedia Inc., a production of
    WGBH Boston — DVD, 2008.
All about Electricity — Schlessinger Media — DVD, 2003.
Biography: Thomas Edison — A & E Home Video — DVD, 2006.

Experiment: Why does a rubber ball or balloon stick to a wall after being rubbed in human hair?

Materials

- Rubber balloon or light-weight, hollow ball
- Human volunteer with hair
- Empty wall space

Process

Rub the rubber ball/balloon through human hair and immediately stick it to the wall.

Science behind the Experiment

Staying on the wall is caused by the electrostatic force. When the ball is rubbed in the hair, electrons in the hair transfer to the rubber ball. The negatively charged ball is then attracted to the positive charges on the wall. The ball will remain on the wall as long as the electrostatic force remains stronger than gravity pulling the ball down.

Experiment References
Gunderson, P. Erik. *The Handy Physics Answer Book*. p 287. Detroit, MI: Visible Ink Press.

Discussion

- Who has toured an electric plant?
- Who worked for an electric company?
- How many items in the room can you name that use electricity?

Follow-up reading suggestions

Canby, Edward Tatnall. 1963. *A History of Electricity*. New York: Hawthorn Books.

Davis, Henry B. O. 1983. *Electrical and Electronic Technologies: A Chronology of Events and Inventors from 1900 to 1940*. Metuchen, NJ: Scarecrow Press.

Herbert, Ralph J. with illustrations by Carlance, John. 1986. *Cut Your Electric Bill in Half*. Emmaus, PA: Rodale Press.

References

Energyquest.ca.gov. 2010. Chapter 2: What Is Electricity? Retrieved August 7, 2010.
http://www.energyquest.ca.gov/story/chapter02.html.

Gundersen, P. Erik. 1999. *The Handy Physics Answer Book*. Farmington Hills, MI: Visible Ink Press.

The Franklin Institute. 2010. Ben Franklin's Lightning Rod. Retrieved August 7, 2010. http://fi.edu/learn/sci-tech/lightning-rod/lightning-rod.php?cts=benfranklin-weather-electricity

Steam Power, Steam Engines

Introduction

Steam as a source of energy was discovered by the Greeks in 1 A.D. However its use as a steam engine belongs to inventors Thomas Savery in 1698, Thomas Newcomen in 1705, and James Watt in 1769. Watt is also the man responsible for the words "horsepower" and "watts" as measurements of energy.

The success of the steam engine fueled the industrial revolution. It was used to power agriculture machines, railroad engines, steamboats, and factories.

A steam engine can use wood, coal, or even nuclear energy to heat water and produce steam under pressure. As the steam expands, it is pushed against a piston or turbine. This pressure does the work needed, such as turning the wheels of a locomotive.

Richard Trevithick built a steam engine which he used on December 24, 1801, to power the first locomotive to carry passengers. In 1825, George Stephenson of England built the first steam-blast engine that made steam railroads practical. He built the world's first public railroad that carried passengers 20 miles between Stockton and Darlington, England.

In the United States, the transcontinental railroad united the country on May 10, 1869. At the end of the 1800s, steam-powered trains carried people and freight over 15 rail lines across the nation.

Trivia

Easy

What is the name of the worker who shovels coal into the furnace of a steam engine?

Answer: The fireman.

Challenging
Name a piece of farm equipment run by a steam engine?
Answer: Steam driven pile driver.

Bonus Round
Where was the first steam railroad engine built in America?
Answer: John Stevens demonstrated the first steam locomotive at his home in Hoboken, NJ, in 1826.

Video

American Railroads: the Steam Train Legacy Volume II — Dastar
 presents an MM & V Production — set of seven VHS tapes, 2001.
When Giants Roamed: The Golden Age of Steam — A & E Home Video
 — DVD, 2005.
Steam Engines of the Wabash Railroad — The Randolph Historical
 Society and Magic City Media — DVD, 2006.

Experiment: How does steam produce energy?

If possible seek out members of a steam engine club who may be willing to bring a model steam engine to your facility. If no one is available, you can do the following experiment.

Materials

- Teakettle
- Electric burner/hot pot
- Water
- Pinwheel (make sure the pinwheel moves easily)

Process

Heat water in a teakettle to boiling. As the steam exits the teakettle, position the pinwheel to be hit by the steam. The steam will make the pinwheel spin. This demonstrates how steam energy works.

Experiment References

Created by Gloria Hoffner.

Discussion

- Who has ridden on a train pulled by a steam engine?
- Did anyone ever work with steam engines?
- Did anyone ever ride on a steamboat?

Further reading suggestions

Avery, Derek. 2002. *One Hundred Years of Steam Trains*. London, England: Canton Editions.

Burton, Anthony. 2000. *Traction Engines: Two Centuries of Steam*, Edison, NJ: Chartwell Books.

Stever, Dean. 1996. *The Golden Age of Steam*. New York: Smithmark.

References

Bellis, Mary. 2010. Outline of Railroad History. Retrieved August 17, 2010. http://inventors.about.com/library/inventors/blrailroad.htm

Brian, Marshall. 2010. How Steam Engines Work. Retrieved August 7, 2010. http://science.howstuffworks.com/transportation/engines-equipment/steam.htm

Ferguson, Rebecca. 2006. *The Handy History Answer Book*. Canton, MI: Visible Ink Press.

Science and Technology Department of the Carnegie Library of Pittsburgh. 1997. *The Handy Science Answer Book*. Farmington Hills, MI: Visible Ink Press.

Coal

Introduction

Coal is the world's most abundant energy source. It is made from the decayed remains of plants buried millions of years ago and compressed by heat and pressure from the Earth.

For thousands of years, humans have burned coal as an energy source for heating homes and in more recent times for powering trains and generating electricity. The U.S. Energy and Information Agency said the need for coal is predicted to grow by more than 40 percent from 2001 to 2025.

Fifty-two percent of America's coal comes from Pennsylvania, Kentucky, and West Virginia. Thirty percent of the U.S. coal reserves are located in Alaska mostly near the Arctic Circle. Other states with coal are Illinois, Arkansas, Kansas, Louisiana, Mississippi, Missouri, Oklahoma, Texas, and Wyoming.

There are two ways for mining underground coal: room and pillar and longwall.

When using room and pillar the coal is removed by cutting large tunnels underground using surrounding coal to support the tunnel roofs. The longwall method takes slice of coal over an extensive section of ground.

Most coal mining in the United States is via the room and pillar process. In England, the longwall method is the most prominent process.

Trivia

Easy
What color is coal?
Answer: Black

Challenging

Why did coal miners take a canary with them into the mine?

Answer: Prior to computers and air quality monitors, miners took birds into the mines as a way to check the air quality. Distress in the bird indicated the presence of dangerous levels of methane, carbon dioxide, or carbon monoxide in the mine.

Bonus Round

When did most coal form?

Answer: Geologists think high-grade coal was formed about 250 million years ago.

Video

Coal Country — Evening Star Productions — DVD, 2009.

Burning the Future: Coal in America — Docurama Films; Paradox
    Entertainment Group; a film by David Novack — DVD, 2008.

Historic Mining & Blasting Industry Films: Coal, Copper, Salt, and Iron
    — Quality Information Publishers, Inc. — DVD, 2005.

Experiment: How does coal form?

It will take six weeks for the process described in this experiment. Begin with the coal science program, keep the experiment in a public area for viewing, and show the results at the next Science for Seniors program.

Materials

- Two-liter soda bottle with the top two inches cut off so you have a straight-sided cylinder
- Medium-grain sand to cover two inches in the soda bottle
- Twigs
- Plant leaves
- Mud
- Sheet of plastic wrap
- Water

Process

Prior to the experiment:

Line the soda bottle bottom with plastic wrap. Pour in about five inches of water. Add two inches of sand and top with twigs and leaves. Wait two weeks and add two inches of mud. Wait two more weeks and drain the water. Wait a final two weeks and after it is dry lift the entire set of materials in the plastic out of the soda bottle bottom.

During the experiment:

Remove the plastic and break the contents in half to show the beginnings of coal formation.

Science behind the Experiment

This simulates how coal formed in the Earth from the remains of plants and animals, heat, pressure, and time. In this experiment, placing mud on the twigs shows the effect of heat and pressure.

Experiment References

Teachcoal.org 2010. Coal Formation. Retrieved August 20, 2010. http://www.teachcoal.org/lessonplans/coal_foundation.html.

Discussion

- Did anyone work in, live near, or visit a coalmine?
- Did anyone ever use coal to heat their homes?
- What are the advantages of the fuels that have replaced coal as energy sources?

Further reading suggestions

Freese, Barbara. 2003. *Coal: A Human History*. Cambridge, MA: Perseus Pub.

Haugen, David M. 2008. *Coal.* — Detroit, MI: Greenhaven Press.

Riddle, John. 2002. *Coal Power of the Future: New Ways of Turning Coal into Energy*. New York: Rosen Pub. Group.

References

Alberta Energy. 2010. What is Coal? Retrieved August 7, 2010.
http://www.energy.gov.ab.ca/coal/645.asp.

Carnegie Library of Pittsburgh. 1997. *The Handy Science Answer Book.*
Farmington Hills, MI: Visible Ink Press.

Economy Watch. 2010. Types of Fossil Fuels, Petroleum, Coal, Natural
Gas, Different Sources of Fossil Fuels. Retrieved August 7, 2010.
http://www.economywatch.com/fossil-fuels/types.html.

King, Byron W. 2009. How Much Coal is Out There? Retrieved August
7, 2010. http;//www.energybulletin.net/node/48240.

Solar Power

Introduction

Solar energy is produced by the sun's rays. The rays can be converted into heat and other forms of energy, including electricity. Each year the Earth receives more solar energy than ten times the energy of the entire planet's supply of fossil fuel.

Tapping into and using solar energy as a source of power has a long history. In the 1800s, British astronomer John Herschel built a thermal box to collect solar energy and used it to cook food.

There are two forms of solar energy: passive and active. Passive solar energy is a process of designing structures that work naturally as energy savers. For example, adobe homes absorb heat during the day and release it during the night with no added mechanical device. Active solar energy means collecting solar energy through a device and using controls to release the energy as needed.

Active solar energy is used today as a way to generate electricity, to heat hot water, and/or supply heat for an entire building. Solar energy is converted to electricity in two ways. One way is by using photovoltaic devices from small ones on a handheld calculator to large panels on a roof to collect and convert sunlight into electricity. In the second way, solar thermal collectors heat a fluid that produces steam and the steam powers a generator to create electricity at a power plant. These large-scale solar power plants are in several states including California, Arizona, and Nevada.

The United States is not the only country installing solar energy systems. Solar panels adorn the roofs of four million Japanese buildings and two-thirds of all homes in Israel.

Solar energy is found everywhere the sun shines. It is not a consistent source of energy due to changes in how sunlight strikes the Earth. These variables include weather, time of day, and season of the year.

Trivia

Easy
You can buy a solar hot water heating system for your house — true or false?
Answer: True

Challenging
What is the sunniest city in the United States?
Answer: Yuma, AZ, has about 4000 hours of sunlight each year.

Bonus Round
How long does it take for sunlight to reach the Earth?
Answer: It takes about 8.4 minutes for light to travel from the sun to the Earth.

Video

Saved by the Sun — WGBH Video — DVD, 2007.
Toward a Better Life, No. 7: Solar Energy: 1980 — National Archives and Records Administration — DVD, 2008.
Solar Energy — Hope for the Future — Increase Video — DVD, 2008.

Experiment: How can you use the sun for cooking?

Materials

- Large clean jar with a lid
- Four tea bags
- Two quarts of water
- Sunny patio or windowsill

Process
Fill the jar with water, Place the tea bags in the jar. Secure the lid. Place in a sunny location for three to four hours. If you serve the tea to residents, do so within 24 hours to avoid bacterial growth. Never use tea that is cloudy or syrupy as it may be a sign of bactcria.

Science behind the Experiment

The tea flavor will seep into the water and the sunlight will heat the water. This demonstrates the heating power of the sun.

Experiment References

Lachlei, M.B. 2010. Directions for Sun Tea. Retrieved July 17, 2010. http://www.ehow.com/how_6511072_directions-sun-tea.html.

Discussion

- Have you ever had food cooked by the sun?
- Have you used solar power for heating water or your home?
- What other forms of energy compete best with solar power in terms of cost, efficiency, and ease of use?

Further reading suggestions

Berinstein, Paula. 2001. *Alternative Energy: Facts, Statistics and Issues.* Westport, CT: Oryx Press.

Butti, Ken and Perlin, John. 1980. *A Golden Thread: 2500 Years of Solar Architecture and Technology.* New York: Van Nostrand Reinhold.

Leggett, Jeremy. 2009. *The Solar Century: The Past, Present and World-Changing Future of Solar Energy.* London: Green Profile.

References

Darling, David. 2004. *The Universal Book of Astronomy from the Andromeda Galaxy to the Zone of Avoidance.* Hoboken, NJ: John Wiley and Sons Inc.

Gunderson, P. Erik. 1999. *The Handy Physics Answer Book.* Farmington Hills, MI: Visible Ink Press.

Wind

Introduction

The winds blowing over the Earth are caused by the sun's uneven heating of the Earth's surface. Uneven heating happens because different land surfaces and water absorb the sun's heat at different rates.

In daylight hours, the air over land heats up faster than the air over water. Warm air rises and cooler air fills in the lower levels of the atmosphere and these reactions are what we call wind. In the evening, the process reverses.

Wind power as an energy source has been used in windmills for centuries. A modern use for wind power is to create large wind turbines. As wind passes through the turbines it turns the blades and generates electricity. As with solar energy, wind energy is dependent on the consistency of blowing wind to generate electricity.

In 2008, wind machines in America generated 52 billion kilowatt hours of electricity. This is only about 1.3 percent of the electricity needed in the U.S. However, it was enough to provide electricity to 4.6 million households. Electricity generated by wind power doubled from 2006 to 2008. In January 2010, President Obama endorsed a new program that would direct $2.3 billion in tax credits for companies that create new solar or wind generating plants.

Trivia

Easy

What country consumes the most energy?
Answer: The United States uses about 42.6 percent of the world's energy.

Challenging

What appliance in your house uses the most electricity?

Answer: A water heater uses 4,219 kilowatt-hours. Other high usage appliances are air conditioners, refrigerators, freezers, and ranges.

Bonus Round

How much energy would you save switching from incandescent to fluorescent light bulbs?

Answer: An 18-watt fluorescent bulb reduces the coal needed to produce energy by 80 percent equal to reducing carbon dioxide into the atmosphere by 250 pounds.

Video

Sixty Minutes: T. Boone Pickens — CBS — DVD, 2008.

Modern Marvels: Renewable Energy — A & E Home Video — DVD, 2008.

Energy Alternatives: Cool Fuel Roadtrips, Wind and Micro Hydro Power — Discovery Education — DVD, 2007.

Experiment: How does wind power work?

Materials

- Pinwheels
- Whirligigs — If possible one in which there is action, such as a figure of a person cutting wood. One source of whirligigs is http://www.hccwhirligigs.com. Books are also available for instructions on making your own whirligigs.
- Fan

Process

Place these items on a lawn area near a window on a windy day. Let the residents observe how the wind moves the shaft that powers the figure cutting wood on the whirligigs. If no wind is present, a fan can be used to power the whirligigs.

Science behind the Experiment
The wind moves these lawn ornaments is the same way in which wind moves giant windmills. The energy generated is used as a power source.

Experiment References
Created by Gloria Hoffner.
Whirligig design: Lunde, Anders. 2003. *Action Whirligigs: 25 Easy-to-Do Projects*. Mineola, NY: Dover Publications

Discussion

- Have you ever seen a wind farm?
- Have you ever seen a windmill working on a farm?
- Do you think wind power will be used in the future as a widespread energy source?

Further reading suggestions

California Office of Appropriate Technology. 1983. *Common Sense Wind Energy*. Andover, MA: Brick House Pub. Co.
Putnam, Palmer Cosslett. 1982. *Putnam's Power from the Wind*. New York: Van Nostrand Reinhold.
Wolf, Ben and Meyer, Hans. 1978. *Wind Energy*. Philadelphia: Franklin Institute Press.

References

Energy Kids. 2010. Renewable Wind. The National Energy Education Development Project. Retrieved August 7, 2010. http://www.eia.doe.gov/kids/energy.cfm?page=wind_home-basics-k.cfm.
Pepitone, Julianne. 2010. Obama unveils $2.3 billion for clean energy jobs. Retrieved August 25, 2010. http://money.cnn.com/2010/01/08/news/economy/green_manufacturing_jobs/index.htm

Hydro Power

Introduction

Water has been a source of power for centuries. The first known dams were built in 3000 B.C. in a place that is now Jordan. It is believed this early dam was used for irrigation.

There are several kinds of dams, but only the hydropower dam is used to generate electricity. It does this by using the difference in water levels to turn a turbine that generates electricity.

Waterfalls are also sources of hydroelectric power. The name for the distance the water drops at a waterfall is called the head. A higher waterfall creates a greater head. However, there are not enough waterfalls to make this a practical source of energy.

Instead we build dams to create artificial waterfalls. Water stored behind the dam increases the head. A dam built across a valley creates a head equal to the height of the dam.

The powerhouse to collect the energy is usually built at the foot of the dam. In the powerhouse are turbines whose blades are turned by the force of the rushing water and the turning blades power electrical generators.

Hydroelectric dams can also be used to store energy. During high-use periods, energy is supplied by water leaving the reservoir. During low-use periods, energy from other sources can be used to pump water back into the reservoir. The water that is pumped back can be used later to produce power.

Some dams store generated power in batteries until needed at high-energy consumption times, but pumping water back into the dam is one of the most efficient ways to store energy. Hydroelectric dams are also useful in a power grid because the can be switched on and off much more easily than coal-fired or natural gas-fired generators.

Trivia

Easy

What is the largest hydroelectric plant in the U.S.?
Answer: The Grand Coulee Dam on the Columbia River in Washington State is the largest hydroelectric plant in the United States.

Challenging

What is the tallest dam in the U.S.?
Answer: Oroville in California is 755 feet tall. It is number 16 on the list of world's tallest dams.

Bonus Round

What is the largest dam in the world?
Answer: The Three Gorges Dam on the Yangtze River in China. It is capable of generating 22,500 megawatts of power. To construct the huge dam, the Chinese government was forced to relocate 1.5 million people living in the valley where the dam was built.

Video

Building Big: Dams — WGBH Boston — DVD, 2004.
China's Mega Dam — Engineering Marvels — Discovery
    Communications — DVD (no date).
Three Gorges: The Biggest Dam in the World — Discovery Channel —
    DVD (no date).

Experiment: How can water be used to create power?

Materials

- Water
- Low tray to collect water
- Child's water wheel toy with gears turned by flowing water

Process

Set the water toy on a table. Ask how many residents have seen a working water wheel? Next put the wheel on the tray and pour the water over the wheel.

Science behind the Experiment
The force of the flowing water turns the wheel and generates power.

Experiment References
Created by Gloria Hoffner.

Discussion

- Who has been to a dam?
- Who has been to a waterfall?
- Did anyone ever work for a hydroelectric company?

Further reading suggestions

Hunt, Bernice Kohn. 1997. *Water Tamers of the World*. New York: Parents Magazine Press.

Kelly, James E. and Park, William R. 1977. *The Dam Builders*. Reading, MA: Addison-Wesley.

Leslie, Jacques. 2005. *Deep Waters: The Epic Struggle Over Dams, Displaced People and the Environment*. New York: Farrar, Straus and Giroux.

References

Funk and Wagnalls, Inc. 1986. *The New Encyclopedia of Science*. Milwaukee, WI: Raintree Publishing Inc.

History of Dams. 2010. United States Society on Dams. Retrieved August 21, 2010. http://www.usdams.org/ussdmenudata.html.

Tucci, Paul A. and Rosenberg, Matthew T. 2009. *The Handy Geography Answer Book*. Detroit, MI: Visible Ink Press.

U.S. Geological Society. 2010. How Dams Work: Water Science for Schools. Retrieved August 21, 2010. http://ga.water.usgs.gov/edu/hyhowworks.html

Chapter 5 — Space

Space — the final frontier. Many of us remember when Apollo 11 landed on the moon in 1969. That great step for mankind opened up a Pandora's box of questions and opened the door for scientific discoveries. This chapter covers everything from astronauts' suits to what would happen if the sun no longer existed. It discusses the craters on the moon, and how scientists discover new planets outside our solar system just by using the theory of gravity. This chapter is filled with out-of-this-world experiments that the scientist in you is sure to enjoy.

The Sun and Other Stars

Introduction

Our solar system consists of one star we call the sun and eight planets. Scientist believe it formed 4.5 billion years ago when a swirling cloud of gas and dust known as a nebula had a chain reaction that resulted in gravity pulling together the sun. Remaining dust and particles were pulled together in a similar fashion to form the planets and moons.

Our sun burns hydrogen and helium. Scientists predict it will continue to burn hydrogen and helium for about another four billion s. When its hydrogen fuel is exhausted and the sun is burning just lium, the sun will swell to three times its current size. As the sun's mass expands, it will destroy Mercury and Venus, the two innermost planets closest to the sun.

Next, it will send solar flares out that will reach the Earth. This will cause the Earth's oceans to boil and rip the atmosphere from our planet. The expanded sun may also rip the Earth apart. Scientists are unsure if the Earth will be torn into pieces due to a gravitational tug between the sun and the Earth or if Earth will become a cold, burnt, barren hunk of rock floating in space.

After the sun becomes a red giant, it will burn for about another billion years. Our sun will eventually shrink down to the size of the Earth and become a white dwarf star.

Supernovas happen only to large stars and occur about once every 50 years in our galaxy. Like all stars, supernovas burn hydrogen and helium, However, when a supernova exhausts these fuels the core heats up and becomes denser. There is a resulting implosion that bounces off the core and expels the remaining stellar matter into space. The discharge of stellar matter we observe is a supernova. What remains after a supernova becomes a neutron star.

Trivia

Easy
What is the Latin name of our sun?
Answer: Sol.

Challenging
What is a solar eclipse?
Answer: When the moon passes in front of the sun blocking all or part of the sun's light from reaching Earth.

Bonus Round
Is it safe to observe a solar eclipse?
Answer: The National Aeronautics and Space Administration (NASA) reports it is safe to view a full eclipse with the naked eye for a brief few seconds. It is never safe to view a partial eclipse with a naked eye. This is because even with 99 percent of the sun covered by the moon, the remaining photospheric crescent is bright enough that it may cause permanent eye damage.

Video

Core Astronomy — Ambrose Video — DVD, 2007.
The Universe: Season One — A & E Home Video — DVD, 2007.
The Dimming Sun — NOVA — DVD, 2006.

Experiment: How will the sun end?

Materials

- A red and a yellow balloon
- Straight pin
- Globe
- Volunteer to blow up a balloon

Process

Blow up the yellow balloon, hold the end closed but do not tie shut — just pinch the bottom with your fingers. Now have a resident hold the globe as you release the air from the yellow balloon so the air passes over the globe. This shows how the sun will rip the atmosphere from the Earth.

Next, blow up the red balloon. Tie it shut. Hold it up and remind residents this is a stand-in for a large red star, larger than our sun. It is far off in space and will end in a supernova explosion. Pop the balloon with the pin to simulate the explosion.

Science behind the Experiment

The air flowing from the yellow balloon over the globe represents what will happen if the sun increases in size and sends out solar flares that will rip the atmosphere from the Earth. (This will not happen for a very, very long time.) Our sun will not explode like a supernova because it is too small. The red balloon represents the end of a supernova, a star about eight to 15 times the mass of our sun.

Experiment References

Created by Gloria Hoffner.

Discussion

- Who has visited a planetarium?
- Who has seen the stars through a telescope?
- Who has seen a solar eclipse and the corona of the sun?

If possible — you could ask who would like to visit a planetarium and/or invite members of a local astronomy club to set-up telescopes at your facility so your residents can enjoy a closer look at the stars.

Further reading suggestions

Cooke, Donald A. 1985. *The Life and Death of Stars*. New York: Crown.

Golub, Leon and Pasachoff, Jay M. 2002. *Nearest Star: The Surprising Science of Our Sun*. Boston: Harvard University Press.

Smithsonian Exposition Books. 1981. *Fire of Life: The Smithsonian Book of the Sun*. New York: Norton.

References

Darling, David. 2004. *The Universal Book of Astronomy*. Hoboken, NJ: John Wiley and Sons Inc.

Mitton, Simon and Jacqueline. 1995. *The Young Oxford Book of Astronomy*. Oxford: Oxford University Press.

Shaffer, Rick. 1994. *Your Guide to the Sky*. Los Angeles: RGA Publishing Group, Inc.

Earth Seasons

Introduction

Have you ever wondered why some parts of the world, such as North America, experience four seasons while in others, such as along the equator, the temperatures remain close to the same all year long?

Our home planet, Earth, is part of solar system of one sun and eight planets. Pluto was downgraded to a dwarf planet on August 24, 2006, by the International Astronomical Union. Earth is the third planet from the Sun beyond Mercury and Venus.

The eight planets orbit the sun. For the Earth, one full trip around the sun equals one Earth year.

Earth has an axis. This is best understood as an imaginary line passing through the Earth from the North to the South Pole. The Earth rotates on its axis once every 24 hours.

As the Earth orbits the Sun, the Earth's axis is tilted at an angle of about 23.5 degrees. During winter in the northern hemisphere the Earth is tilted so that the North Pole is pointed away from the Sun and the South Pole is pointed towards the Sun.

In summer in the northern hemisphere, the situation is reversed with the Earth tilted so the North Pole is tilted towards the Sun and South Pole is tilted away from the Sun.

The result: in the winter the North receives direct sunlight at a very low angle and thus does not receive as much solar energy as during the summer months.

Why is it always cold at the North and South poles? Even though the sun shines 24 hours a day during the summer at the poles, it never gets higher than 23.5 degrees above the horizon. At that low angle it does not deliver much energy. Even so, the temperatures at the poles can warm up to about freezing (32 degrees) in mid-summer. During the winter, the sun never shines. It gets much, much colder. Temperatures in the winter can be lower that -45 degrees. The temperature difference between summer and winter is about 77 degrees.

There is no land mass at the North Pole. Instead, ice formed on the surface of the Arctic Ocean never fully melts. In the South Pole, where there is land, over the centuries the ice and snow have built up, forming ice caps and glaciers.

One place on the Earth where temperatures remain constant is the equator. The equator is an imaginary circle running about 25,000 miles around the Earth. It is located equally between the North and South Poles. The Amazon, African, and Indonesian rainforests are located on the equator.

The average temperature at the equator is between 80 and 90 degrees when the altitude is near sea level. There are a constant 12 hours of daylight and 12 hours of night at the equator because of how the sunlight strikes this central location on the Earth.

At the equator, the temperature remains about the same throughout the year, however, temperatures in cities near the equator vary.

For example: Singapore in China is located 1 degree north latitude from the equator. It has a hot, humid climate with a temperature in the 80s. Quito, Ecuador sits almost directly on the equator and yet has spring type weather and sometimes the temperature dips as low as 25 degrees.

The difference is due to elevation. The highest point in Singapore is 538 feet above sea level while Quito, in the Andes Mountains, is over 9,200 feet above sea level. The higher elevation is the reason Quito has a cooler climate than Singapore.

Trivia

Easy
What color is our sun?
Answer : yellow

Challenging
What is the Latin name of our Earth?
Answer: Terra

Bonus Round

One third of all stars are in binary systems — two stars in the same system. Some scientists have speculated there may be a second sun in our solar system located about three light years away. What is the name of this sun?

Answer: Nemesis.

Video

Planet Earth: Pole to Pole, Mountains and Deep Ocean — BBC — DVD, 2007.

Planet Earth, the Complete BBC Series — BBC Warner — five DVD boxed set, 2007.

Disney Nature Earth — Walt Disney Studios Home Entertainment — DVD, 2009.

Experiment: Why do some parts of the Earth experience seasons, while in other locations the weather is the same all year long?

Materials

- Flashlight
- Globe
- Darkened room
- Two volunteers (Volunteer one must be able to hold the globe and walk unassisted around volunteer two who will stand holding the flashlight

Process

As volunteer one walks around volunteer two, volunteer one keeps the globe tilted at about 23 degrees, with the North Pole always pointed to the same corner of the room. That's how the Earth orbits the sun, with the North Pole always pointing the same way in space. Specifically, the North Pole always points toward the North Star.

In one part of the orbit the beam from the flashlight will hit above the equator and more directly on the northern hemisphere of the globe.

This represents summer in the north. Now have volunteer one keep walking around volunteer two so the beam hits the southern hemisphere more directly. This represents winter in the north.

Science behind the Experiment

The flashlight represents the sun. The volunteer circling the globe and shining the flashlight demonstrates the changes in how the sunlight strikes the northern and southern hemisphere during the year. It also illustrates that even though the Earth is tilted so the sun hits more on the northern or southern hemisphere, it always casts the same light on the center of the globe, the equator.

Experiment References

Created by Gloria Hoffner.

Discussion

- Has anyone ever lived, worked, or visited a location on the equator?
- Has anyone traveled near the North or South Pole?
- Would you rather live in a place that has seasons or a place where the weather is about the same all year?

Further reading suggestions

These selections are reflections by humans on the change of seasons and not the science facts of the change of seasons.

Mother Earth News. 2009. *The Mother Earth News Almanac: A Guide Through the Seasons.* Topeka, KS: Mother Earth News.

Pluckrose, Henry and photos by Faircloud, Chris. 1993. *Changing Seasons (Walkabout)* New York: Franklin Watts Ltd.

Stuzt, Bruce. 2008. *Chasing Spring: An American Journey through a Changing Season.* New York: Scribner.

References

Engelbert, Phillis and Dupuis, Diane L. 1998. *The Handy Space Answer Book.* Detroit, MI: Visible Ink Press.

Science for Seniors

Wisegeek. 2010. What is the Equator? Retrieved July 29, 2010.
    http://www.wisegeek.com/what-is-the-equator.htm.

Astronauts

Introduction

Humans have viewed the stars from Earth for centuries. In the 20th century, men and women rocketed into space and landed on the moon.

On April 12, 1961, Yuri Gagarin, of the U.S.S.R., became the first human in space. The 27-year-old orbited the Earth for 108 minutes. He is reported to have said of his experience, "I see the Earth. It is so beautiful."

He was followed into space by American Alan Shepard on May 5, 1961, in a suborbital flight. Shepard returned to space in 1971 as commander of the Apollo 14 mission where he became the fifteenth man to walk on the moon.

On February 20, 1962, American John Glenn orbited the Earth for 4 hours and 55 minutes. He was the fifth man to orbit the planet. By 2010, 508 individuals, 456 men, and 52 women from 38 countries had flown into space.

Unlike the heroes of science fiction who fly quickly from planet to planet without fear of ship malfunctions or illness as a result of space travel, real-life space travel carries many dangers. When the first astronauts launched into space there was a real fear they would suffer eye damage and other physical problems due to the intense pressure from the rocket pulling free of the Earth's gravity. This problem proved untrue; however the concerns about radiation in space and the effects of long-term weightlessness remain.

Space suits are designed to keep astronauts safe in space. They are designed to provide life support in space. They contain: air, water, a communication system, and a heating or cooling system. They are puncture resistance for micro matter flying through space and the suit also provides for waste disposal.

For space walks and space repairs, the astronauts practice wearing space suits on Earth while they are submerged in water to simulate weightless conditions.

In 1978, NASA lifted age restrictions and the prohibition against women astronauts. The requirements are height between 5' 3" and 6' 3", be in excellent physical condition and hold a degree in engineering, biology, physical science, or math.

Trivia

Easy
Who was the first American in space?
Answer: Alan Shepard.

Challenging
Who was the oldest American to fly into space?
Answer: John Glenn was age 77 when on October 29, 1998, he returned to space on Space Shuttle Discovery, mission STS-95. On this trip he spent nine days in space.

Bonus Round
What country sent the first woman into space?
Answer: Valentina Vladimirovna Nikolayeva Tereshkova of the U.S.S.R. was the first woman to travel in space. Flying the Vostok 6, she orbited the Earth for three days, June 16 through June 19, 1963. The first American woman in space was Sally Ride. On June 18, 1983, she orbited the Earth on Space Shuttle Challenger.

Video

When We Left Earth: The NASA Missions — Discovery Channel — set of four DVDs, 2008.
Space Station IMAX — Toni Myers director — DVD, 2005.
From Earth to the Moon Signature Edition — HBO Home Video — three box set of DVDs, 2005.

Experiment: How does it feel to wear a space suit?

Materials

- Two men's winter jackets — one large and one extra large
- Newspaper
- Two pairs of men's thick gloves — one pair larger than the other
- A large wing nut and a matching screw mounted on a board

Process

Prior to the experiment:

Place the smaller jacket inside the larger jacket and fill the space between the jackets with crumbled newspaper. Do the same with the gloves.

During the experiment:

Ask a resident to volunteer as the simulated astronaut. Suit up the resident in the jacket and gloves. Now ask the resident to attempt to attach the wing nut to the screw.

Science behind the Experiment

Space suits are bulky and weigh about 310 pounds. Wearing a simulation space suit demonstrates the difficulty astronauts face working in space. In addition, working in space, astronauts must make sure not to tear their suit because exposure to space results in death in less than 60 seconds due to the complete vacuum. The astronaut cannot retrieve a dropped screw or tool because in space there is so little gravity that the dropped object would simply float away. For this reason also, astronauts are attached to the spacecraft with air hoses providing oxygen in space.

Experiment References

Created by Gloria Hoffner.

Discussion

- Who wanted to be an astronaut?
- Has anyone visited a NASA center such as the Kennedy Space Center in Florida, the Goddard Visitor Center in Maryland, the

Johnson Space Center in Houston, and/or George C. Marshall Space Flight Center in Alabama?

- Has anyone ever met an astronaut?

Further reading suggestions

Aldrin, Buzz. 2009. *Look to the Stars*. New York: Putnam Juvenile.

Jones, Thomas D. 2007. *Skywalking: An Astronauts Memoir* New York: Harper Paperbacks.

Mullane, Mike. 2007. *Riding Rockets and Other Outrageous Tales of a Shuttle Astronaut*. New York: Scribner.

References

Cernan, Eugene. 2000. *The Last Man on the Moon: Eugene Cernan and America's Race in Space*. New York: St. Martin Griffin.

Ferguson, Rebecca. 2006. *The Handy History Answer Book*. Detroit, MI: Visible Ink Press.

NASA. 2010. NASA History in Brief. Retrieved August 2, 2010. http://history.nasa/gov/brief.html.

The Moon

Introduction

The moon is about 4.5 billion years old. Where the moon came from has been debated by astronomers over the centuries. Share these theories with the residents and let the residents guess which one they feel is correct.

1) The moon was wandering in the solar system and was pulled into orbit with the Earth by Earth's gravity.
2) The moon formed as the solar system and planets formed.
3) The moon was formed when an object hit the forming and spinning Earth and a chunk of the newly formed planet was detached thus creating the moon.

The most widely believed theory is number three. Astronomers believe the moon was formed when the newly formed planet Earth was struck by a rogue planet. This impact theory states the debris from the collision eventually condensed into the moon.

Located about 238,900 miles from the Earth, the moon has a diameter of 2,160 miles. The force of gravity on a space object's surface is determined by the mass and size of the object. Gravity on the moon is 1/6th the gravity felt on the Earth. For example, if you weigh 132 pounds on Earth, you would weigh 22 pounds on the Moon.

Everyone who has looked at the moon at night searching for the Man in the Moon is aware that the moon has many craters. These were formed by the impact of meteors and comets colliding with the moon.

On July 20, 1969, when Neil Armstrong and Buzz Alden landed on the moon, the craters were a serious concern. There was a fear that the spacecraft would fall into a crater or drop into heavy layers of meteor dust. Armstrong was able to guide the craft to a safe area and, as they say, the rest is history.

During NASA's manned moon missions, the astronauts brought 842 pounds of moon rocks back to Earth.

Trivia

Easy
What happened to the lunar crafts the astronauts rode on the surface of the moon?
Answer: The rovers remain on the moon.

Challenging
What happened when astronaut David Scott dropped a feather and a hammer on the moon at the same time?
Answer: They landed at the same time. This demonstrated Galileo's 300-year-old theory that in the absence of air resistance, all objects fall at the same rate.

Bonus Round
On the moon, it is easier than on Earth to lift an object due to less gravity. Is it also easier to move an object from side to side?
Answer: No, it would be the same as on Earth. Gravity creates a vertical pull, but the force needed to move an object depends on its mass, which is not the same thing as weight.

Video

In The Shadow of the Moon — Velocity/ThinkFilm — DVD, 2008.
The Universe: The Complete Season Four — A & E Home Video —
    Three disc set; disc one contains: The Day the Moon Was Gone —
    DVDs, 2004.
Essential Space Collection — The Discovery Channel, includes Base
    Camp Moon. — DVD, 2009.

Experiment: Why does the moon have craters?

Materials

- Glass baking pan 13" x 10"
- White flour, 2" deep in pan
- Paprika powder
- Small rocks and pebbles

Process

Fill the pan two inches deep with flour. Shake paprika over the flour until the surface of the flour is covered. Have a resident toss a small pebble into the flour. Let the residents see how the pebble throw up small bits of flour and creates a crater. Let other residents throw small rocks creating their own craters and observing how these change the surface of the "moon."

Science behind the Experiment

Craters formed the pockmarked surface of the moon. Similar craters formed on Earth but they have been eroded by wind, vegetation, and water. Many of the small meteors that would create a crater on the moon never reach the Earth because they are burned up in the atmosphere. One of the largest exposed Earth impact craters is the Barringer crater in Arizona which is more than 700 feet deep and 4,000 feet wide.

Experiment References

Created by Gloria Hoffner.

Discussion

- Who remembers the expression, "The moon is made of green cheese?"
- Who remembers the excitement of watching the moon landings?
- What do you think about people who doubt that man really landed on the moon and say it was a hoax by the U.S. government?

Further reading suggestions

Cosner, Sharon. 1990. *Lunar Bases*. New York: F. Watts.

DeGroot, Gerald J. 2006. *Dark Side of the Moon: The Magnificent Madness of the American Lunar Quest*. New York: NYU Press.
Stroud, Rick. 2009. *The Book of the Moon*. New York: Walker & Company.

References

Light, Michael. 1999. *Full Moon*. New York: Alfred A. Knopf.
Maran, Stephen P. PhD. 2005. *Astronomy for Dummies*. Hoboken, NJ: Wiley Publishing Inc.
National Geographic. 2004. Moon Facts. Retrieved August 7, 2010. http://news.nationalgeographic.com/news/2004/07/0714_0404714_moonfacts.html
Space.com. 2009. The Reality of Life in Orbit by Robert Z. Pearlman. Retrieved April 4, 2009.
http://www.space.com/php/spacetrivia/index.php?quiz=Orbit.
The New Universe, Here, Now and Beyond. National Geographic Magazine Time Life Specials. Washington, DC. Published August 5, 2010.

Mars

Introduction

Mars is the fourth planet from the sun. It is about half the size of Earth, but has a longer year, since it takes Mars 687 days to orbit the sun.

Living conditions on Mars are not like on Earth. Mars is a barren planet with dust storms, little oxygen, and very frigid temperatures. During the day the planet can reach a high of -20 degrees and at night drop to -120 degrees.

There was a time when humans believed there was life on Mars. These theories began when Gian Domenico Cassini discovered that Mars had polar caps that increased in the winter and decreased in the summer. Giovanni Schiaparelli discovered dark markings on the Martian surface he called canali or channels in 1877. Some people then speculated the canals might be channels dug by intelligent life on Mars and used as irrigation for Martian vegetation.

These theories were joined by a 1970s theory that aliens built a sphinx-like structure called The Face on Mars. The face is actually a collection of Martian landscape in the Cydonia region of Mars which when photographed by the Viking spacecraft in 1976, gave the appearance of a human face. NASA later determined this was a natural landform.

The face and canal theories of life on Mars were eliminated by the findings of numerous Soviet and American robotic spacecraft which since the 1960s, have scanned, photographed, and landed robots on the planet without finding any trace of life.

However, Mars was once a warmer and wetter planet so scientist hold out hope that perhaps there is some single-cell life at a very early stage living underground on the red planet.

Trivia

Easy
Where does Mars get its name?
Answer: It is named for the Roman god of war because of its red coloring.

Challenging
What was the first spacecraft to travel to Mars?
Answer: In 1962 the Soviet Union became the first nation to send a spacecraft to Mars. It was called Mars 1 and failed to achieve an orbit around Mars.

Bonus Round
How long would it take someone to travel from Earth to Mars?
Answer: When the planets are closest in orbit, about every 25 months, it would take 214 days in a conventional rocket to reach Mars. A nuclear rocket could make the trip in about four months.

Video

Roving Mars —Buena Vista Entertainment — DVD, 2007.
Eyes on Mars — Space Holdings — DVD, 2003.
NOVA — Mars Dead or Alive — WGBH Boston — DVD, 2004.

Experiment: What physical changes happen to astronauts during space travel?

Materials

- Jar with lid
- Vinegar
- Two turkey/chicken leg bones

Process
One month prior to the Science for Seniors program:
Clean the bones. Place one bone in a jar of vinegar and seal the lid. Store the second bone in a clean dry place.

Day of the program:
Place the jar and the clean bone side by side on a table. Remove the bone from the vinegar. Allow residents to feel both bones. The bone softened by the vinegar represents bones weakened by weightlessness.

Science behind the experiment
Scientists estimate a trip to Mars would be about nine months to Mars, about four months exploring the planet, and about nine months back to Earth. In the weightlessness of space, astronauts on average lose one to two percent of bone mass per month. NASA is working to find ways to keep astronauts' bones strong and healthy in space.

Experiment Reference
NASA. 2001. Space Bones. Retrieved February 4, 2012.
 http://www.science.nasa.gov/science-news/science-at-nasa/2001/ast01oct_1/

Discussion
- Who would like to travel to Mars?
- Who believes there is intelligent life on other planets?
- Do you think humans will ever set up colonies on Mars?

Further Reading Suggestions
Simon, Seymour. 2000 *Destination Mars*. New York: Morrow Junior Books.
Zubrin, Robert. 2008. *How to Live on Mars: A Trusty Guidebook to Surviving and Thriving on Mars*. New York: Three Rivers Press.
Zubrin, Robert and Wagner, Richard. 1996. *The Case for Mars: The Plan to Settle the Red Planet and Why We Must*. New York: The Free Press.

References
Cain, Frasier. 2008. Universe Today. How Long Does It Take to Get to Mars? Retrieved August 17, 2010.

www.universetoday.com/14841/how-long-does-it-take-to-get-to-mars/.

Carlotto, Mark. 1997. *The Martian Enigmas: A Closer Look: The Face, Pyramids and Other Unusual Objects on Mars*. Berkeley, CA: North Atlantic Books.

Darling, David. 2004. *The Universal Book of Astronomy*. Hoboken, NJ: John Wiley and Sons, Inc.

NASA. 2001. Unmasking the Face on Mars. Science. Retrieved August 18, 2010. http://science.nasa.gov/science-news/science-at-nasa/2001/ast24may_1

NASA. 2010. Planets. Retrieved August 2, 2010. http://www.nasa.gov/worldbook/planet_worldbook_update.html.

The Astronomical Society of the Pacific. 1993. *The Face on Mars by Sally Stephens*. Issue 25.

Pluto

Introduction

Pluto was discovered in 1930 by Clyde W. Tombaugh at the Lowell Observatory in Flagstaff, AZ. It is named for the Roman god of the underworld.

Located at the edge of the solar system, the surface of Pluto could not be seen by an Earth telescope at the time of discovery. In 1996, the Hubble Space Telescope showed Pluto to have ice at the polar regions and unknown bright and dark spots on the surface. From this scientist speculate Pluto's temperature ranges from a high of about -350 degrees to a low of about -380 degrees.

In 1978, astronomers discovered that Pluto, which is only about 1,500 miles in diameter, had a moon. The moon was named Charon which is a little over half the diameter of Pluto, making it the largest moon to planet ratio in the solar system.

As Earth and space telescopes improved, astronomers discovered more moons around Pluto. They also discovered over 70,000 objects in the Kuiper Belt, a region of space at the edge of the solar system that may contain material left over from the formation of the solar system. Objects in the Kuiper Belt appear to have the same composition as Pluto, which is located in the Kuiper Belt. Astronomers have also discovered other planetary type satellites that, like Pluto, have moons.

Astronomer Mike Brown discovered a new solar object in 2005 which is located farther away from the sun than Pluto. Named Eris it is about 1,600 miles in diameter with 25 percent more mass than Pluto.

In 2006 the International Astronomical Union downgraded Pluto to the status of a dwarf planet. This association of professional astronomers set the following standards for planet status: it must orbit the sun, it needs sufficient gravity to be a spherical shape, and it needs to be a dominant gravitational body. Pluto failed the last requirement.

Trivia

Easy

After the discovery of Pluto, Walt Disney named a character after the planet. Who is this character?
Answer: Pluto, Mickey Mouse's dog.

Challenging

What does Pluto have in common with Earth?
Answer: A moon.

Bonus Round

When will we have close-up images of Pluto?
Answer: The New Horizons Spacecraft mission of NASA is expected to arrive at Pluto in 2015 and send back images of the dwarf planet.

Video

A Traveler's Guide to the Planets — National Geographic Video — two
    DVD set, 2010.
Journey to the Edge of the Universe — National Geographic Video —
    DVD, 2009.
Cosmic Journey: The Voyager Interstellar Mission and Message — A &
    E Home Entertainment — DVD, 2009.

Experiment: How does Pluto orbit the sun?

Materials

- 10 Styrofoam balls of different sizes: the sun the largest, Pluto the smallest
- 10 paper clips
- String
- Marker

Process

Label and/or color the balls to represent the sun, eight planets, and Pluto.

Option 1: Suspend the balls representing the planets from the ceiling of the room of the science program. This can be done by bending paper clips into hangers for tiled ceilings.

Option 2: Have residents volunteer to hold the balls at various locations around the room. Distribute the balls with the Sun in the center of the room. Place the other planets around the room starting outward from the sun in this order: Mercury, Venus, Earth, Mars, Jupiter, Saturn, Uranus, and Neptune. Do not hang Pluto. Instead, walk Pluto on its orbit around the sun, once in front of Neptune and then once behind Neptune to show how unlike the other planets in our solar system, Pluto's elliptical orbit has much more difference between its closest approach to the sun and its farthest approach.

Science behind the Experiment

Pluto has a very unusual elliptical orbit from 30 astronomical units (each unit equals one measurement of distance from the sun to the Earth) to 39 astronomical units. For this reason, Pluto sometimes is closer to the sun than the planet Neptune and other times Neptune is closer to the sun. It takes Pluto 248 years to make one full orbit around the sun.

Experiment References

Created by Gloria Hoffner.

Discussion

* Do you remember when Pluto was discovered?
* Do you remember hearing or reading in the news when Pluto was demoted to a dwarf planet?
* Do you think Pluto should have remained a planet?

Further Reading Suggestions

Boyle, Alan. 2009. *The Case for Pluto: How a Little Planet Made a Big Difference.* Hoboken, NJ: Wiley.

Scott, Elaine. 2007. *When Is A Planet Not A Planet?: The Story of Pluto.* New York: Clarion Books.

Tyson, Neil deGrasse. 2009. *The Pluto Files: The Rise and Fall of America's Favorite Planet*. New York: WW Norton Company.

References

Cain, Fraiser. 2008. Orbit of Pluto. Retrieved August 22, 2010. http://www.universetoday.com/13865/orbit-of-pluto/.

Engelbert, Phillis and Dupuis, Diane L. 1998. *The Handy Space Answer Book*. Detroit, MI: Visible Ink Press.

NASA. 2010. Pluto. Retrieved August 8, 2010. http://www.nasa.gov/worldbook/planet_worldbook_update.html.

Tyson, Neil deGrasse. 2009. *The Pluto Files: The Rise and Fall of America's Favorite Planet*. New York: WW Norton Company.

Universe Today. 2008 UnicWhy is Pluto Not a Planet? Retrieved July 29, 2010. http://www.universetoday.com/2008/04/2010/why-pluto-is-no-longer-a-planet/.

Exoplanets

Introduction

Throughout most of history, scientists believed our solar system was unique in the universe because of the presence of planets. Contrary to science fiction, working astronomers did not believe there were planets orbiting other suns.

In 1992, astronomers discovered a planet orbiting a pulsar star in the constellation Virgo. This began a search for exoplanets, the term for planets outside our solar system, which led to the discovery of hundreds of new planets.

Less than ten years later in 2001, a solar system was found about 123 light years from Earth with a planet seventeen times the size of Jupiter. In 2010, astronomers announced they have discovered over 70 solar systems. On August 25, 2010, astronomers announced the discovery of a solar system 127 light years away with five planets, the most ever found in another solar system. As of January 23, 2012, 728 such planets have been identified

Earth-like planets, perhaps capable of supporting life, have been found by the Kepler Mission. Knowing there are more stars in the universe than grains of sand on the Earth increases the possibility of life on other worlds. Scientists now believe stars have an average of 1.6 planets in orbit around them and that there are even more free-floating planets not attached to stars.

Astronomers look for three signs of an exoplanet: a wobble of a star indicating a planet's gravity is tugging on the star; a shadow from a planet crossing in front of a distant star; and a glow caused by the heat of a newly formed planet.

Frank Drake, a professor emeritus of astronomy and astrophysics at the University of California, Santa Cruz, developed an equation to test for the possibility of life on other planets. He believes finding intelligent life on another world depends not only on finding a planet capable of supporting life. Drake believes we must also find a planet with a technically evolved civilization capable of sending a message or responding to a message from us and also locating that civilization while they still exist. He allows for the possibility that an advanced civilization may have existed and is now extinct on a far distant planet.

Trivia

Easy
What planet in our solar system is called Earth's twin?
Answer: Venus because it resembles Earth in size and mass. However, it has a surface temperature of about 870 degrees.

Challenging
How do astronomers find new planets?
Answer: In searching deep space the astronomers watch for changes in a star's movement caused by the slight gravitational pull on the star due to the presence of a planet. They also look for a shadow crossing in front of a star as a sign of a possible planetary system.

Bonus round
In August and September 1977 the United States launched Voyager 1 and 2 as unmanned probes designed to travel outside the solar system. What was on the probes?
Answer: They carried a chart showing Earth's location in the Milky Way galaxy, a collection of music and sounds, photos, and greetings in 54 languages.

Video

The Universe Season Three — A & E Home Entertainment — DVD, 2009.
Cosmic Voyage — IMAX — DVD, 2002.
Stargaze — Hubble's View of the Universe — DVD International — DVD, 2000.

Experiment: How does gravity help astronomers discover new planets outside our solar system?

Materials

- Orange
- Pebble

Process

Hold an orange in one hand and a pebble in your other hand. Ask the residents which they think will land first and why? Drop both objects to the floor at the same time and observe.

Science behind the Experiment

Both objects land at the same time because gravity pulls on them equally regardless of the weight of the object. The tug of an exoplanet on a star in another solar system is one way astronomers locate new planets.

Experiment References

Created by Gloria Hoffner.

Discussion

- Do you believe there is life on other planets?
- If so, what do you think that life would be?
- Would you like to travel to another planet?

Further reading suggestions

Casoli, Fabienne and Encrenaz, Therese. 2010. *The New Worlds: Extrasolar Planets*. New York: Springer.

Mason, Jason. 2009. *Exoplanets: Detection, Formation, Properties, Habitability*. Berlin, Heidelberg: Springer.

Oliviuer, Marc. 2009. *Planetary Systems: Detection, Formation and Habitability of Extrasolar Planets*. Berlin, Heidelberg: Springer,

Science for Seniors

References

Aero Space Guide. 2010. Extrasolar Planets. Retrieved August 13, 2010.
    http://www.aerospaceguide.net/extrasolar.html.
Atkinson, Nancy. 2010. Exoplanets — as many of seven of them —
    spotted in newfound star system. Retrieved August 25, 2010.
    http://www.csmonitor.com/Science/Cool-
    Astronomy/2010/0825/Exoplanets-as-many-of-seven-of-them-
    spotted-in-newfound-star-system.
Jet Propulsion Laboratory. 2012. NASA's Kepler Announces 11 New
    Planetary Systems. Retrieved January 27, 2012.
    http://www.jpl.nasa.gov/news/news.cfm?release=2012-026
NASA. 2010. Planets. The First Discoveries. Retrieved August 2, 2010.
    http://www.nasa.gov/worldbook/planet_worldbook_update.html.

Space Shuttles

Introduction

The space shuttle, an orbiter that brings materials and people to the International Space Station, was conceived in the 1960s. A shuttle is 184 feet long and can hold eight passengers and cargo. Columbia was the first shuttle. Launched on April 12, 1981, it was followed by the construction of shuttles Challenger in 1982, Discovery in 1985, Atlantis in 1985, and Endeavor in 1991.

The space shuttles are not the same as the early space capsules used by astronauts to reach the moon. Shuttles are winged space planes lifted into space with re-useable booster rockets. They land, like a plane, on a specially designed three-mile runway and have an advantage over the early space capsules by allowing astronauts to move around freely and conduct experiments while onboard.

U.S. space capsules were designed to orbit Earth and some capsules carried men and landing crafts to the surface of the moon. Capsules were one time use only. The space shuttle cannot travel to the moon.

There were two disasters during the space shuttle program and in both tragedies all hands were lost.

The Challenger Space Shuttle blew up during launch on January 28, 1986. NASA's investigation revealed that a leak in a booster rocket caused the explosion.

The Space Shuttle Columbia broke apart during re-entry on February 1, 2003. The explanation was a failure in a heat shield that protects the shuttles from extreme temperature when re-entering Earth's atmosphere.

The space shuttle program ended in 2011.

Trivia

Easy
Who was the first U.S. woman in space?
Answer: Sally Ride onboard the Space Shuttle Challenger on April 4, 1983.

Challenging
What was the name of the space shuttle test model?
Answer: Enterprise. Completed September 17, 1976, it was used for ground and flight tests. It was named for the fictional Starship Enterprise of the Star Trek television and movie series.

Bonus Round
What happened when the U.S. shuttle program ended?
Answer: Astronauts now travel to and from the International Space Station in Russian space capsules.

Video

Space Shuttle, DVD Collectors Set — The Space Store — DVD, 2005.
Columbia Space Shuttle Disaster — WGBH Boston — DVD, 2009
America in Space: The First 40 Years — Finley-Holiday Production — DVD, 2005.

Experiment: How does gravity feel to the astronauts?

Materials
- Punching ball
- Elastic string

Process
Blow up the punching ball and attach the elastic string. Whirl the ball over your head. Have the residents take turns quickly whirling the ball.

Science behind the experiment
The tug on the elastic by the balloon is a representation of the tug of gravity on an astronaut as they leave the Earth.

Experiment References
Singleton, Glen. 2007. *501 Science Experiments. Experiment #4 Gravity.* Heatherton, Australia: Hinker Books Pty Ltd.

Discussion

Further reading suggestions

Ackman, Martha. 2003. *The Mercury 13: The Untold Story of Thirteen American Women and the Dream of Space Flight.* New York: Random House.
Duggins, Pat. 2009. *Final Countdown: NASA and the End of the Space Shuttle Program.* Gainesville, FL: University Press of Florida.
Jenkins, Dennis R. 2001. *Space Shuttle: The History of the National Space Transportation System.* North Branch, MN: Dennis Jenkins.

References

eHistory. 1996. History List: The First 10 People in Space. Smithsonian Guides: Spaceflight. Retrieved July 29, 2010. http://chistory.osu.edu/world/ListPreviewOnly.cfm?LID=6&PrevieOnly=yes&public=yes
Space.com. 2009. The Reality of Life in Orbit. Retrieved April 9, 2009. htt:p//www.space.com/php/spacetrivia/indexes.php?quiz=Orbit.

Eclipses

Introduction

A lunar eclipse happens when the Earth passes between the sun and the moon and the Earth's shadow falls on the moon. This happens only during a full moon. It does not occur every full moon. This is because the plane on which the moon orbits the Earth tilts at about five degrees when compared to the path of the Earth around the sun.

A lunar eclipse occurs when there is an alignment of the Earth, Moon, and Sun. A lunar eclipse can last all night and can be seen from anywhere on the Earth where it is nighttime.

A solar eclipse occurs when the moon gets between the Sun and the Earth preventing sunlight from striking the Earth. This can form a total or partial blocking of the sun's rays. They last only a few minutes.

A partial solar eclipse is visible somewhere on Earth between two and five times a year. A total solar eclipse happens about 1½ times each year.

Ancient civilizations associated eclipses with coming doom. The Chinese believed a dragon was consuming the sun. Scientific research has shown there is no danger to humans from the event of an eclipse. However viewing a solar eclipse before and after it reaches totality — where the sun is completely covered — can lead to serious eye damage. It is important to view it only with a special filter. Dark glasses are not sufficient to prevent eye damage. Even during totality it is safe to view the eclipse for only a few seconds.

Trivia

Easy

How many times bigger is the Sun than the Moon?
Answer: The sun's diameter is 400 times that of the moon. If the moon were 140 miles less in diameter a total solar eclipse would not occur.

Challenging

How often does a total solar eclipse happen in the same location?
Answer: About once every 370 years.

Bonus Round

Will there be a time when there are no total eclipses?
Answer: Yes. The orbit of the moon is pulling away from the Earth a little bit each year while the sun is also increasing in size. Scientists estimate in about 600 million years the distance between the Earth and the Moon and the size of the sun will eliminate the Moon's ability to completely cover the Sun's disk.

Video

The Story of the Total Eclipse — Duke Video — DVD (1999).
What Is an Eclipse — Phoenix Learning Group, Inc. — DVD.
Total Eclipse in the Arctic — Discovery — video slide show on a
    website as filmed by Dave Moocher, producer for Discovery Space,
    who walks you through his trip to a total 2008 solar eclipse as seen
    from the North Pole. The site is http://dsc.discovery.com/space/
    slideshows/total-solar-eclipse-slideshow.html.
Discovery News site with photos from a solar eclipse over Asia on July
    22, 2009: http://dsc.discovery.com/news/slideshows/solar-eclipse-
    asia.html.

Experiment: What causes an eclipse?

Materials

- Tennis ball
- Ping-pong ball
- Room that can be darkened
- Flashlight
- Table

Process

Place a tennis ball on a table about 24 inches from a flashlight. Darken the room. While shining the flashlight on the tennis ball, move the ping-pong ball around the tennis ball between the tennis ball and the flashlight.

Science behind the Experiment

The tennis ball represents the Earth, the ping-pong ball represents the Moon, and the flashlight represents the Sun. The shadow cast by the ping-pong ball represents a solar eclipse.

Experiment References

Singleton, Glen. 2007. *501 Science Experiments*. Heatherton, Australia: Hinker Books Pty Ltd.

Discussion

- Who has seen an eclipse?
- Did an eclipse scare you as a child?
- Would you like to see an eclipse?

Further reading suggestions

Harrington, Philip S. 1997. *Eclipse: What, When, and How Guide to Watching Solar and Lunar Eclipses*. New York: Wiley.

Littman, Mark. 1999. *Totality: Eclipses of the Sun*. New York: Oxford University Press.

Pasachoff, Jay M. 1993. *The Cambridge Eclipse Photography Guide: How and Where to Observe and Photograph Solar and Lunar Eclipses*. Cambridge, MA: Cambridge University Press.

References

Engelbert, Phillis and Dupuis, Diane L. 1998. *The Handy Space Answer Book*. Detroit, MI: Visible Ink Press.

Satellites

Introduction

Sputnik, the first artificial satellite, flew into space on October 4, 1957. Built by the Soviet Union, Sputnik was the size of a basketball and weighed 183 pounds. It flew around the Earth in 98 minutes. This small craft started the space race because the United States feared the U.S.S.R., a cold war enemy, would be capable of launching rocket attacks from space.

Unknown in the earliest part of the space race, commercial satellites would change the way the world communicates. On July 10, 1962, American Telephone and Telegraph launched Telstar 1, the first commercially funded satellite. Telstar 1 was able to transmit voice, data, and television signals. Its first transmission, an image of an American flag flying in the breeze, was sent from the United States to England. Today, orbiting satellites are used for military observations, weather forecasting, television transmissions, telephone calls, crop monitoring, and much more.

Long before the invention of satellite phones and global positioning systems, Arthur C. Clarke, scientist and science fiction writer, predicted that an artificial satellite placed in orbit at the equator would orbit the planet at the same time and direction as the Earth rotates on its axis. This is called a geosynchronous orbit in which the satellite is placed about 22,300 miles above the Earth.

Clarke's idea is used today in many navigational and communication satellites because of a stable orbit and large coverage area. This space equator belt is now called the Clarke belt.

Trivia

Easy

Can a baseball be hit so high and hard that it will orbit the Earth?
Answer: Only if hit by Superman. The baseball would have to travel at a velocity of 17,800 miles per hour.

Challenging

How does a satellite stay in orbit?
Answer: An object orbits the Earth as long as it has enough horizontal velocity. Because there is no air resistance in space, when a satellite reaches the correct balance between speed and gravity, it retains a stable orbit.

Bonus Round

How fast would a satellite have to be traveling if it was accidentally shot out of Earth's orbit?
Answer: It would have to travel 25,000 miles per hour to travel into interplanetary space.

Video

Satellites — The History Channel — DVD, 1997.
Sputnik Mania — The History Channel — DVD, 1997.
NASA 25 Years — Madacy Video Imprint — DVD, 1998.

Experiment: How did Sputnik stay in orbit?

Materials

- Small bucket
- ½ bucket of water
- Two feet of rope
- Four large towels

Process

Place the towels on the floor. Tie the rope to the handle of the bucket. Fill the bucket half full of water. Swing the bucket fast around your body.

Science behind the Experiment

The water stays in the bucket due to momentum. The water wants to keep going in a straight line and the bucket holds it in. A satellite stays in orbit around the Earth due to the balance between gravity holding the satellite to the planet and its velocity pulling it away.

Experiment References

Created by Gloria Hoffner.

Discussion

- Who remembers the launch of Sputnik?
- Who remembers their first cell phone?
- What sort of space program should the U.S. have in the future?

Further Reading Suggestions

Graham, Ian. 2001. *Satellites and Communication*. Austin, TX: Raintree
    Steck-Vaughn.
Hilvert, John and Bruce, Linda. 2005. *Communications Technology*
    North Mankato, MN: Smart Apple.
Long, Mark and Keating, Jeffery. 1983. *The World of Satellite
    Television*. Summertown, TN: Book Pub. Co.

References

Ferguson, Rebecca. 2006. *The Handy History Answer Book*. Detroit, MI:
    Visible Ink Press.
NASA. 2007. Sputnik and the Dawn of the Space Age. Retrieved
    October 5, 2007. http://history.nasa.gov/sputnik/

Space Probes

Introduction

A probe is an unmanned craft sent into space to gather information. Some probes fly past the sun, moon, and planets capturing photo images and sending data back to Earth. Other probes orbit a planet or asteroid and some even land on the surface, explore, and return samples for scientists to study.

The first space probe was the Soviet Union's Luna 2 landing on the surface of the moon in 1959, Space probes have also been launched by the United States, the European Union, Japan, China, and India. Memorable moon probes include the Soviet Luna 3, which took the first photos of the far side (commonly referred to as the dark side) of the moon in 1959, and the seven U.S. Surveyor probes, five of which successfully photographed possible landing sites for the Apollo moon landing.

Between 1965 and 1968, the U.S. launched a Pioneer series of probes to study the sun. In 1970, the Soviet Luna 16 successfully sent the first samples of moon dust to the Earth and Luna 17 put the first roving vehicle on the moon.

It was 1967 when the Soviet Union launched Venera 4 which reached Venus and transmitted information for 94 minutes before being crushed by the atmosphere of the planet. In 1974 and 1975 the U.S. probe Mariner 10 collected photographic images and information about the planets Mercury and Venus.

In 1976 U.S. probes Viking 1 and Viking 2 both made successful landings and transmitted information on Mars. Launched in 2003, NASA Mars rovers, Spirit and Opportunity, landed on the planet's surface in 2004. Spirit stopped transmitting in March 2010, but Opportunity continued to send signals as of January 2012.

The NASA Cassini probe to Saturn and Titan, the planet's largest moon, was launched in 1997. It was still sending data to Earth as of

January 2012. The U.S. Mars Curiosity probe was launched in November 2011 and is expected to land on the planet in August 2012.

Trivia

Easy
Who was president in 1977 when NASA launched Voyager 1 and 2?
Answer: Jimmy Carter, who along with then U.N. Secretary Kurt Waldheim, recorded a message of greetings to whoever may someday find the probe.

Challenging
What was the path of the Voyager probes?
Answer: Voyager 1 traveled to Jupiter and Saturn. Voyager 2 toured Saturn, Uranus, and Neptune. Both probes were then directed into deep space.

Bonus Round
How long will the Voyagers materials survive?
Answer: Each probe contains a gold plated record, needle, and instructions on how to play the device housed in a protective aluminum shield. It is designed to last 40,000 years, the time NASA estimates it will take the probes to reach another planetary system.

Video

Planets: New Discoveries — American Educational Products — DVD (no date).
Are We Alone in the Universe? — UFO TV — DVD, 2003.
The Planets — New Video Group — DVD, 1999.

Experiment: How far has the Voyager 1 space probe traveled since its launch in 1977?

Materials

- 100 sheet roll of toilet paper
- Color markers

Process

Space is so vast even the size of our solar system seems hard to comprehend. This brings the dimension to the residents in a simple and measurable way.

Bring the roll of toilet paper and markers to the residents seated in a row against the long wall of a room. On the first sheet of toilet paper have a resident draw a circle and write Mercury, the planet closest to the sun.

Roll 1.8 sheets and hand the roll to the next resident who should draw Venus. The third resident, at 2.5 sheets into the roll, draws and labels Earth. Next is Mars at 3.8 sheets, followed by Jupiter, all the way at 13.2 sheets, and then Saturn at 24.2 sheets. Skip a few residents and then land at Uranus at 48.6 sheets, followed by Neptune at 76.3 sheets, and the last resident is the dwarf planet Pluto a long 100 sheets away from Mercury.

Science behind the Experiment

One sheet of toilet paper equals about 35.5 million miles. Voyager 1 and Voyager 2 were launched by NASA in 1977 and sailed past Pluto into deep space about 1990.

Experiment References

Beatte, Rob. 2007. *101 Incredible Experiments for the Weekend Scientist*. p 123. New York: Metro Books.

Discussion

- Do you remember when Voyager 1 and 2 were launched?
- Do you think the probes will reach another planetary system?

- Do you think anyone will ever find the probes and accept an invitation to visit our planet?

Further reading suggestions

Burgess, Eric. 1982. *By Jupiter: Odysseys to a Giant.* New York: Colombia University Press.

Cooper, Henry S. F. 1983. *Imaging Saturn: The Voyager Flights to Saturn.* New York: Holt, Rinehart and Winston.

Davis, Joel. 1987. *Flyby: the Interplanetary Odyssey of Voyager 2.* New York: Athenaeum.

References

Engelbert, Phillis and Dupuis, Diane L. 1998. *The Handy Space Answer Book.* Detroit, MI: Visible Ink Press.

Mitton, Simon and Jacqueline. 1995. *The Young Oxford Book of Astronomy.* New York: Oxford University Press.

NASA. 2012. Cassini: Unlocking Saturn's Secrets. Retrieved February 4, 2012. http://www.nasa.gov/mission_pages/cassini/whycassini/cassini2012011.html

NASA. 2012. Mars Science Laboratory in Good Health. Retrievcd February 4, 2012.
http://www.nasa.gov/mission_pages/msl/news/milestones.html

Chapter 6 — Oceans

The ocean covers over two-thirds of the surface of the planet we live on, so is it any wonder that the ocean is the subject of so many experiments and discoveries? Scientists can explain some things with solid science such as what makes seashells hard or how the moon affects the tides, but they are still trying to figure out for sure how water came to earth. And did you know the first submarine was made in 1620? Read through this chapter and find out all about the ocean!

Ocean Formation

Introduction

The history of Earth's oceans begins about 3.8 billion years ago when our planet was a very hot rock without any liquid water. As the planet formed, gases where released from the Earth's molten core due to volcanic activity.

These gases included methane, ammonia, water vapor, and carbon dioxide. Water vapor was produced and remained in a gaseous state until the planet cooled. As the planet cooled, the water vapors became rain and the rain pooled on low-lying lands to form the first oceans.

Water in the Earth's oceans may have also come to the planet through comets and meteorites. Comets are called "dirty snowballs" because they are objects made of ice, dust, and rock that orbit the sun in an egg-shaped orbit. As they orbit the sun, the comets heat up, melting gases and water, thus leaving a visible vapor trail called a tail. In the process, the comets lose some mass with some of the water and dust particles flying out into the universe.

Comets have also struck the Earth and other planets in both ancient and modern times. In July 1994, astronomers observed the Comet Shoemaker-Levy 9 slam into Jupiter. There is speculation that comets striking the Earth during the early days of the planet brought water and chemicals compounds including carbon dioxide, methane, and ammonia that helped to form Earth's oceans.

To show that materials from comets may be part of the origin of the oceans we can compare a comet's make-up to what is in our oceans. The European space mission Rosetta is heading towards the comet Churyumov-Gerasimenko. The Rosetta is expected to arrive near the comet in 2014. The orbiting craft will launch a lander called Ptolemy to test for chemicals on the comet seeking to find if the chemical make up on the comet matches the chemicals found in Earth's oceans.

Trivia

Easy

How many planets in our solar system have known oceans of water?
Answer: Only Earth.

Challenging

Where else in the solar system do scientists think there may be water?
Answer: Scientists believe water may be frozen under the surface of the moon or Mars.

Bonus Round

Where in our solar system is there the possibility of a frozen ocean?
Answer: Europa is a moon of Jupiter discovered by Galileo in 1610. Astronomers have observed ice covering the entire moon, making them speculate on the possibility of a liquid ocean beneath the ice.

Video

Ocean Origins — Gerald Calderon-Razor Studios — DVD, 2008.
Ocean Origins — IMAX — DVD, 2005.
Earth — The Biography — National Geographic — DVD, 2008.

Experiment: Did comets bring water to Earth?

Materials

- Water
- Dirt
- Ice cube tray (one that makes round ice if possible)
- Warming tray
- Clear 10" x 13" baking pan
- Paper cups

Process

Prior to the experiment:

Make a tray of "comet" ice cubes by placing small amount of dirt in a container and fill the remainder with water in each compartment. Freeze.

During the experiment:

On the day of the program, put a layer of dirt on the bottom of the baking pan. Give each resident a frozen cube in a paper cup. Have the residents roll the cubes in the dirt to create the exterior of the comet. Put the cubes back in the paper cups. Level out the remaining dirt in the pan.

Place the baking pan of dirt on a warming tray. Have the residents toss their "comet" ice cube into the tray one at a time.

Science behind the Experiment

The dirty ice cubes represent comets. The baking pan on a warming tray represents the hot, forming Earth. The comets melt, flow into the irregular surface, and contribute to the oceans and waterways of the planet.

Experiment References

Created by Gloria Hoffner.

Discussion

- What ocean is closest to your facility?
- Who has visited, lived, or worked near the ocean?
- What are your ocean memories?

Further reading suggestions

Levy, H. 1998. *Comets: Creators and Destroyers*. New York: Simon and Schuster.

Redfern, Ron. 2001. *Origins: The Evolution of Continents, Oceans and Life*. Norman, OK: University of Oklahoma Press.

Wegener, Alfred. 1966. *The Origin of Continents and Oceans*. Dover, DE: Dover Publications.

References

Astrobiology. 2003. Europa: Frozen Oceans in Motion. Retrieved August 2, 2010. http://www.astrobio.net/exclusive/688/europa-frozen-ocean-in-motion.

Bennett, Jeffrey; Donahue, Megan; Schneider, Nicholas; Voit, Mark. 2000. *The Cosmic Perspective*. San Francisco: Addison Wesley Longman, Inc.

Duke. 2010. How Did the Oceans Form? Retrieved August 2, 2010. http://www.chem.duke.edu/jds/cruise_chem/oceans/ocean1.html.

Kidseclipse.com. 2010. How Does a Comet Movc? Retrieved August 2, 2010. http://www.kidseclipse.com/pages/a1b3c0d4.html.

Natural History Museum. 2010. How Did the Solar System Form? Retrieved July 28, 2010. http:/www.nhm.ac.uk/nature-online/space/planets-solar-system/formation/index.html.

NASA. 2004. How the Planets Formed: NASA — Planets. Retrieved August 2, 2010. http://www.nasa.gov/worldbook/planet_worldbook_update.html.

Ocean Tides

Introduction

The Earth's ocean tides are caused by the gravitational pull of the moon. As the moon orbits the Earth, the moon pulls strongest on the water when the oceans face the moon. Another tidal bulge occurs on the side of the earth away from the moon because the moon pulls the earth away from the water. High tides occur about 12½ hours apart.

The sun's gravity also influences the tides, however since the sun is much further away, it has about half the pull of the moon. The tidal effects of the sun are also about half of the effect of the moon.

A spring tide does not happen in the spring. Rather it refers to the tides that occur during a full moon or a new moon when the gravitational pull of the sun and the moon come together and result in the highest tides.

A neap tide is the time of the smallest tides. It occurs when the sun, moon, and Earth form a right angle. This happens during the first and last quarters of the moon.

Tides have a connection to the weather. During a storm, the combination of strong winds and high tides can increase coastal flooding.

Trivia

Easy
Are lakes affected by tides?
Answer: Most lakes do not have enough water to visibly show the gravitational pull of the sun or the moon. However, in a large lake such as Lake Superior there is a visible tide fluctuation of about three inches.

Challenging
Does the moon affect the air?
Answer: Yes. The moon's gravity creates a slight change in the air pressure on the Earth.

Bonus Round

How does the gravity of the moon change the shape of the Earth?
Answer: The moon and the Earth pull each other into an egg-like shape because the gravitational force is larger on one part of the object than on the other parts.

Video

The Universe Season Four — A & E Home Video studio — DVD, 2010.
Drain the Ocean — National Geographic — DVD, 2010.
Oceans, Coasts and Tides — Educational Video Network, Inc. — DVD, 2004.

Experiment: How does the Moon affect Earth's oceans?

Materials

- 10" x 13" clear baking pan
- Water
- Empty paper tube
- Tape
- Plastic drinking straw
- Blue food coloring
- Felt-tip permanent marker
- Scissors

Process

Cut the straw to about the same height of the pan. Tape the straw to one side of the pan on the inside. Take the paper tube and tape it to the outside of the pan on the same side as the straw, making sure that when you look through the paper tube, you can see the straw. Fill the pan with water and add food coloring. Mark the water level on the straw. Next gently lift one side of the pan. When you tilt the pan to one side, and then the other, make sure each time to mark the straw to indicate water level.

Science behind the Experiment

The water in the pan represents the Earth's oceans. The pull of the moon's gravity on the Earth creates high and low tides. The markings on the straw show how the water level changes with the tides.

Experiment References

Nye, Bill. 1999. *The Great Big Book of Science Featuring Oceans and Dinosaurs*. New York: Hyperion Books for Children.

Discussion

- Did you ever stand on the beach during high or low tide?
- Have you ever been in a storm during high tide?
- What have you found on the beach at the tide line?

Further Reading Suggestions

Clemons, Elizabeth. 1967. *Waves, Tides and Currents*. New York: Knopf.

Rogers, Daniel. 1991. *Waves, Tides and Currents (The Sea)*. New York: Bookwright Press.

Whipple, A.B.C. and the editors of Time Life Books. 1984. *Restless Oceans*. London: Time Life Books.

References

Bennett, Jeffrey; Donahue, Megan; Schneider, Nicholas; Voit, Mark. 2000. *The Cosmic Perspective.* San Francisco: Addison Wesley Longman.

Engelbert, Phillis and Duane, Diane L. 1998. *The Handy Space Answer Book*. Detroit, MI: Visible Ink Press.

Hile, Kevin. 2009. *The Handy Weather Answer Book*. Detroit, MI: Visible Ink Press.

Water Density

Introduction

Why do some things float and others sink? The answer is density. An object will float when it weighs less than the amount of water it displaces. Everyday examples of this science fact are boats. An empty boat floats on the water because it weighs less than the amount of water it displaces. If you put enough people and cargo into the boat, you can add more weight than the displacement of the boat and it will sink. This is why boats carry warnings not to exceed a maximum number of passengers.

Another example of this principal is a life preserver. A cubic foot of the foam used in life preservers weighs one pound while a cubic foot of water weighs 62 pounds. Because of this, every cubic foot of foam in a life preserver can support 61 pounds. It is important to note that life preservers are built to accommodate weights of children and adults. A large adult may sink in a child's life preserver because the weight of the person may exceed the amount of buoyancy provided by the life preserver.

A way to make a heavy object float is to change the composition of the water. Salt water in the ocean is about 2.5 percent heavier than the same amount of fresh water; this is due to the weight of the salt. Therefore, things a little too dense to float in fresh water will float in salt water.

The Dead Sea, located on the border of Jordan and Israel, is 35 percent salt. The average salt level in the world's seas is 3.5 percent. This high level of salt increases the density of the water making it extremely easy for people to float on the Dead Sea.

Due to this high level of salt, the water in the Dead Sea is deadly to fish. There are two reasons the Dead Sea is so salty. First, it is fed by rivers and streams that bring mineral salts into the water. Second, the Dead Sea is landlocked so it cannot empty the mineral salts. Because it is located in a very warm climate, water in the Dead Sea evaporates, leaving the mineral salts behind.

Trivia

Easy
What two oceans lie on either side of the contiguous continental United States?
Answer: Atlantic and Pacific.

Challenging
What large body of water is off the coast of Alaska?
Answer: The Bering Sea.

Bonus Round
What is the world's largest ocean?
Answer: The Pacific Ocean. It covers about 69,375,000 square miles or 35% of the earth. It is almost as big as the other four oceans combined.

Video

Discover Planet Ocean — Living Arts — DVD, 2010.
Blue Planet: Sea of Life, Special Edition — BBC Warner — DVD, 2007.
IMAX Coral Reef Adventure — Image Entertainment — DVD, 2004.

Experiment: What is the density difference between fresh and salt water?

Materials

- Two clear glasses
- Water
- Salt (3 Tablespoons)
- Fresh egg
- Hardboiled egg
- Spoon or some object to remove the egg from the glasses

Process

In one glass add water and salt; fill the second glass with just water. Place the glasses where the residents can see both glasses. Ask the residents if they think that the fresh egg will float in the two different cups. After the answer, place the eggs in one cup and then the other. The egg in the saltwater will float. Do the same with the hard-boiled eggs.

Science behind the Experiment

This difference is due to the higher density of the salt water. An object floats when it is less dense than the water it displaces. Salt water is denser than fresh water thus an object that sinks in fresh water can float in salt water. It is safe to eat both eggs.

Experiment References

Reeko Scientist. 2010. Floating Eggs in Salt Water. Retrieved February 18, 2010.
http://www.reekoscience.com/Experiments/FloatEggInSaltwater.asp x

Discussion

- Who has used a life jacket?
- Who has traveled to a lake, an ocean, or the Dead Sea?
- Who has noticed the difference between swimming in fresh water and salt water?

Further reading suggestions

Suplee, Curt. 1996. *Everyday Science Explained*. Washington, DC: National Geographic Society.
Trefil, James S. 1983. *The Unexpected Vista: A Physicists View of Nature*. New York: Scribner.
Von Baeyer, Hans Christian and illustrations by Hartman, Laura. 1984. *Rainbows, Snowflakes and Quarks: Physics and the World around Us*. New York: McGraw-Hill.

References

Anderson, Larry. 2010. How Does a Life Preserver Work? August 2, 2010. ehow.com

Extreme Science. 2010. Why Is It Called The Dead Sea? Retrieved August 2, 2010. http://www.extremescience.com/zoom/index.php/earth-records/37-dead-sea.

Tucci, Paul A. and Rosenberg, Matthew T. 2009. *The Handy Geography Answer Book*. Detroit, MI: Visible Ink Press.

Sailing the Seven Seas

Introduction

Our planet is called Earth, but about 71 percent of the planet's surface is covered by the ocean. More than 50 percent of the ocean is over 9,800 feet deep.

There are five oceans:

1) The Pacific, the largest ocean, separates Asia and Australia from North, Central, and South America. It is 69,375,000 square miles and makes up almost half of all oceans.

2) The Atlantic, the second largest ocean, is 41,105,000 square miles, or 21% of the earth. This separates the Americas from Eurasia and Africa.

3) Third largest is the Indian Ocean which covers 28,900,000 square miles, or 15% of the earth. Its waves lap against southern Asia and it separates Africa and Asia.

4) Different from the rest is the Southern Ocean, fourth largest. It covers 7,848,000 square miles, but it does not separate any landmass. It encircles Antarctica and covers much of the Antarctic.

5) The Arctic Ocean is the smallest ocean covering 5,427,000 square miles. Its waters cover much of the arctic and touch the coasts of North America and Eurasia.

The Dead Sea, located between Jordan and Israel, and the Aral Sea, located between Kazakhstan and Uzbekistan, are not oceans because they are landlocked.

Archeologists believe the first humans left Africa in boats and traveled over the ocean over 130,000 years ago. There is evidence of sailing by coastal cultures around the world as a means of expansion for a growing civilization as well as trade with other cultures.

Sailors across the globe used various materials for boat construction including birch bark, balsa wood, papyrus, and ox hide. Once onboard, they used people, rowing, wind power, and machinery as energy for moving the ship.

To navigate, ancient sailors began by rowing out only to the distance where they could still see the coastline. Some archeologists believe, that next they ventured a bit further into open waters relying on scent and clouds by day and the stars at night as navigational references. There are records of sailors charting courses by star points 600 years before the birth of Christ.

Ancient Norse sailors, who lived months without stars, relied on the movements of birds, while the Polynesians used changes in the waves to navigate between islands.

During the Middle Ages sailors used a tool called an astrolabe, a disc of metal suspended by a small ring used to measure the sun's height against the horizon. The sextant, invented in 1731, helped sailors chart their ocean journey by using the stars. Today's sailors have global positioning systems that connect them electronically with orbiting satellites to give an exact position anywhere on the Earth.

In addition to sailing above the water, since the 1500s men have desired to sail under the water in submarines. The German U-Boats of World War I were the first submarine fleet successfully used in battle.

Trivia

Easy
In what book/movie was a submarine attacked by a giant squid?
Answer: *Twenty Thousand Leagues under the Sea* by Jules Verne.

Challenging
What was the name of the first nuclear powered submarine?
Answer: Nautilus (which is the same as the name of Jules Verne's submarine)

Bonus Round
What was the first workable submarine made of?
Answer: In 1620, Dutch scientist Cornelious Van Drebbel made a workable submarine out of a rowboat covered with waterproof skins.

Video

The Great Ships: Submarines — A & E Home Video — DVD, 2006.
Digging for the Truth: The Vikings Voyage to America — A & E
    Entertainment — DVD, 2009.
Man, Moment, Machine: Great Sub Rescue — A & E Home Video —
    DVD, 2010.

Experiment: How does a submarine work?

Materials

- Empty two-liter plastic soda bottle and cap
- Plastic kiddy pool
- Water

Process

Float the empty soda bottle in the kiddy pool. This represents the submarine on the surface of the water. Next remove the cap, fill the soda bottle half full with water and place it in the kiddy pool. It will float at an angle with the part of the bottle underwater showing how ballasts work to hold the ship under the water.

Science behind the Experiment

As a submarine dives, the air is compressed and water fills the metal compartments called ballast tanks. This increases the density of the submarine and it sinks. When the submarine is underwater, air is pumped into the ballast tanks to a mixture that allows the ship to remain and maneuver underwater. To raise the ship back up to the surface, additional air is pushed into the ballast tanks making the ship lighter than the water it is displacing.

Experiment References

Created by Gloria Hoffner.

Discussion

- Who has sailed on the ocean?

- What sorts of positioning systems have you used (GSP, sextant, others)?
- Who has been on a military submarine or tourist submarine?

Further reading suggestions

Anderson, Romola. 1963. *Sailing Ship — Six Thousand Years of History,* 2nd edition. Orange Park, FL: Bonanza Books.

Chapelle, Howard I. with drawings by the author and Wales, George C. and Rusk, Henry. 1988. *The History of American Sailing Ships.* New York: Random House Value Publishing.

Humble, Richard. 1991. *A World War Two Submarine.* New York: P. Bedrick Books

References

Goebel, Greg. 2001. The First Battle of the Atlantic. Retrieved August 3, 2010. http://www.vectorsite.net/twsub2_1.html.

Socyberty. 2010. Our Ancestors, The Sea-farers? Retrieved August 3, 2010. http://socyberty.com/history/our-ancestors-the-sea-farers/.

Tyson, Peter. 2010. Secrets of Ancient Navigation. Retrieved August 3, 2010. http://www.pbs.org/wgbh/nova/longitude/secrets.html.

Whitt, Stephen. 2008. How Does a Submarine Work? Retrieved August 3, 2010. http://www.yesmag.ca/how_work/submarine.html.

Sea Creatures

Introduction

Scientists believe life on Earth began at the bottom of the ocean as microorganisms about four billion years ago. At this time, the surface of the early planet was too hot for life. The oceans would have been cooler and would have shielded the earliest life forms and microbes from intensive radiation.

Today, there are an estimated two million species of marine life including 15,000 species of fish in the ocean. Researchers have discovered fish living up to seven miles deep in the ocean. Deep-sea corals living off the coast of Hawaii are the oldest living sea animals with a skeleton in the ocean.

Corals are marine organisms that live in colonies and have an exterior skeleton. They form coral reefs, such as the Great Barrier Reef in Australia. One Hawaii species, *Leiopathes,* has colonies that have been growing for 4,265 years old, according to a Texas A & M University study published by The National Academy of Sciences in March 2009.

Tales and fears of sea creatures have existed since the first sailors. The giant squid, a sea creature of legend and theme for science fiction books and movies, was photographed by researchers from the National Science Museum of Japan on September 30, 2004. A female giant squid can grow to 43 feet long and males grow 33 feet long. One of the only predators of a giant squid is a sperm whale.

The largest mammal on Earth, the blue whale, lives in the ocean. It measures up to 100 feet long. It is rarely seen and scientists have not been able to learn much about this huge creature.

Great vast areas of the seas, including deep underwater trenches, have never been explored due to their locations. Technology is helping to expand scientist's ability to explore the sea. In July 2010, marine biologists from Australia discovered a six-gilled shark living 4,500 feet beneath the Great Barrier Reef.

Trivia

Easy
What sea creature is chasing boats in the book, *Jaws* by Peter Benchley?
Answer: A great white shark.

Challenging
What is the large mammal living in the ocean that breast-feeds its young?
Answer: A blue whale. The largest found was over 90 feet long.

Bonus Round
What creature is behind the mermaid myth?
Answer: The manatee. A manatee will eat by coming to the surface and pulling vegetation into its mouth. When startled, it will dive suddenly with its tail flapping against the waves. Some believe these actions viewed from a distance created the mermaid myth.

Video

Ocean Wonders, Encountering Sea Monsters, Oceans in Glass: Behind the Scenes of the Monterey Bay Aquarium — Questar — DVD, 2006.

Shark Hunter: Chasing the Great White — Discovery Communications, Inc. — DVD, 2010.

Sea Monsters — A Prehistoric Adventure — National Geographic Video — DVD, 2008.

Experiment: How does a squid protect itself from predators?

Materials
- Tall clear glass vase
- Drawing of a whale
- Food coloring

Process
Fill the vase with water; paste the photo of the whale so the picture can be seen through the vase. Have the residents see the whale through the water. Now tell the residents the squid is in danger and will activate his defenses. Add the food coloring to the water.

Science behind the Experiment
The food coloring represents a squid ejecting ink from their ink sac to fool a predator. In the ocean, the ejected ink comes out in the shape of a squid. The squid turns its body pale and swims away. The whale will go after the ink blob, which looks like the squid it was just chasing, allowing the pale creature, which is the real squid, to swim away.

Experiment References
Created by Gloria Hoffner.

Discussion

- Who has been to an aquarium?
- Who has seen a squid?
- What other sea creatures have you seen?

Further reading suggestions

Conklin, Gladys. 1977. *The Octopus and Other Cephalopods*. New York: Holiday House.
Cousteau, Jacques-Yves and Paccalet, translated by Paris, Mark I. 1988. *Whales*. New York: H. N. Abrams
Wise, William. 1975. *Monsters of the Deep*. New York: Putnam.

References

NASA. 2010. Ocean Planet: In Search of a Giant Squid — How Does a Squid Defend Itself? Retrieved August 5, 2010. http://seawifs.gsfc.nasa.gov/OCEAN_PLANET/HTML/squid_defen d_itself.html

Nye, Bill. 2005. *The Great Big Book of Science featuring Oceans and Dinosaurs*. New York: Hyperion Books for Children.

Thompson Andrea. 2009. Oldest Sea Creatures Have Been Alive 4,000 Years. Retrieved February 2, 2012. http://www.livescience.com/ 3434-oldest-sea-creatures-alive-4-000-years.html

Seashells

Introduction

Seashells are the exoskeletons of mollusks — creatures without an internal skeleton that live in either fresh or salt water. The shell is loosely attached to the mollusk's body and provides protection. Ocean mollusks withdraw fully or partially into their shells when threatened by a predator.

Shells are composed of calcium carbonate. The shell grows with the creature, but not steadily as with the growth of a person. Rather the upper part of the shell is formed from tissue on the mantle edge of the creature. The inside of the shell is formed by tissue from the mantle surface of the creature. For this reason, all shells are a little bit different.

The outer surface of the mollusk shell changes as the creature grows. It can even be repaired by the mollusk. When the mollusk dies, the shell remains. Shells of ocean mollusks wash up on the shore and are called seashells.

Have you ever wondered why there are so many different kinds, shapes, and colors of seashells? This is due to several factors: the type of creature who lived in the shell, the diet of the mollusk, and even the water temperature in which the creature lived. Mollusks in warm waters have a greater variety of food sources and thus produce shells in more colors than cold water dwellers whose limited food sources produce shells in darker shades.

Trivia

Easy

Name a sea creature that lives in a seashell?

Answer: Oysters, clams, or mussels

Challenging

How do farmers use seashells?

Answer: Seashells are ground up and used as fertilizer. They provide the soil with calcium.

Bonus Round

How does an oyster make a pearl?

Answer: An oysters shell has two parts. When a foreign object enters the oyster between t' _ mantel and the existing shell, the foreign object is irritating to the oyster. The oyster solves the irritation problem by covering the foreign object with the same natural material that formed the inside of the shell. The result is a pearl.

Video

ewitness — Shell — D.K. Publishing — VHS, 2007.
Eyewitness — Ocean — D.K. Publishing — DVD, 2007.
Eyewitness — Fish — D.K. Publishing — DVD, 2007.

Experiment: What makes a seashell hard?

Materials

- Two seashells
- Two jars
- Vinegar
- Water

Process

Prior to ι ϵ experiment:

Fill one jar with water and one with vinegar. Place a seashell in each jar and place them in a public area where residents can observe what is happening. In four days, hold the science program and remove the seashells from the jars. Let the residents feel each shell.

Science behind the Experiment

Seashells contain calcium carbonate. Vinegar contains acetic acid. When the seashell is placed in vinegar the calcium carbonate dissolves into a calcium salt and carbonate that bubbles away.

Experiment References

Local 12. 2008. Bendy Bones, Bouncy Eggs, and Squishy Seashells. Retrieved August 5, 2010. http://www.local12.com/content/weather.doppler_tim/story/Bendy-Bones-Bouncy-Eggs.
Modified by Gloria Hoffner.

Discussion

For this topic try to obtain from a store, or as a museum loan, samples of seashells labeled as to type so the residents can hold and examine the shells during the program. One website where you can purchase shells is seashellworld.com.

- Who collected seashells at the beach?
- Who went clam digging?
- What is your favorite beach memory?

Further reading suggestions

Arthur, Alex. 1989. *Shell*. New York: Knopf.
Eiseberg, Jerome M. A. 1989. *Collectors Guide to Seashells of the World*. New York: Crescent Books.
Oliver, A.P. and Nicholas, James. 2004. *Guide to Seashells of the World*. New York: Firefly Books.

References

Atlantic Horticulture. 2010. Seashell Compost. Retrieved August 5, 2010. http://www.atlantichort.com/en/products/compost-soil/sea-shell-compost.html.

How Stuff Works. 2010. How Do Oysters Make Pearls? Retrieved
    August 5, 2010. http://animals.howstuffworks.com/marine-
    life/question630.htm.
Seashell World. 2007. What Are Seashells? Retrieved August 5, 2010.
    http://seashellworld.com/artman/publish/article_4.shtml.

Fresh Water Monsters

Introduction

Visions of the Loch Ness Monster, or Nessie as she is called by her fans, began in the sixth century at The Great Glen, a body of water in the Scottish Highlands 60 miles long, deeper than the North Sea and never known to freeze.

St. Columba, an Irish saint, said he was swimming across Loch Ness to retrieve a boat when a monster appeared swimming alongside him. The saint reported he yelled at the creature and chased it away. Periodic sightings in the water and interest in the mystery of the unknown creature have continued ever since.

The desire to solve the mystery continues with a theory that Nessie is perhaps a dinosaur, a plesiosaur, who escaped extinction. Others believe all the sightings are hoaxes designed to keep a legend alive.

If Nessie exists, the creature may not be alone in the world. Champ, a creature who witnesses say looks a lot like Nessie, is reported to live in Lake Champlain, a very deep lake on the border of New York and Vermont. Like Loch Ness, Lake Champlain is connected to the sea. Champ has access to the ocean via the St. Lawrence Seaway.

In July 1609, French explorer Samuel de Champlain reported seeing a creature 20 feet long with a horse head and serpent body. Since then, more than 300 people have reported seeing a "creature" of various sorts in the lake.

As with Nessie, the speculation is Champ is a plesiosaur who survived extinction. No one has found any remains or physical evidence of either Nessie or Champ.

Trivia

Easy
What is the best evidence that Nessie exists?
Answer: Perhaps the best evidence for Nessie is sonar contacts from Operation Deepscan in 1987. Several photographs have also been taken, but they are all disputed.

Challenging
What is China's lake monster?
Answer: The Lake Tianchi Monster said to live in Heaven Lake near Baejdu Mountain located in a mountain range between China and North Korea.

Bonus Round
What frozen moon may contain water creatures?
Answer: Europa, a moon of Jupiter, appears to be frozen three miles deep and then perhaps contains liquid water.

Video

Sea Monsters: A Prehistoric Adventure — National Geographic — DVD, Blu-Ray, 2007.
The Curse of the Mummy's Tomb; Was There Ever a Monster in Loch Ness; The Mysterious Crashes of the Comet; Have Aliens Ever Landed on Earth? — Madacy Entertainment Group — VHS, 1998.
History's Mysteries: Monsters of the Sea — A & E Home Video — DVD, 2008.

Experiment: How do archeologists put together pieces for solving ancient mysteries?

Materials

- Ceramic mug
- Dishtowel
- Glue
- Plastic bag
- Clear punchbowl
- Food coloring

Process

Prior to the experiment:

Prior to the Science for Seniors program wrap the mug in a dishtowel place in a plastic bag and drop from five feet or higher onto a hard surface, such as a sidewalk or a driveway. Make sure it breaks into several pieces. Drop the pieces into the punchbowl. Add food coloring to make the water murky.

During the experiment:

At the program, bring the punchbowl with the mug pieces into the program room. Ask the residents to guess what they think is in the water. Move the punchbowl to the far end of the room; does the residents' opinion of what is in the bowl change?

Take out the pieces and place them on a dishtowel. Ask the residents to again guess the nature of the object.

Science behind the Experiment

This shows how people can mistakenly identify an object, such as a log on a lake, as something else. It also shows how hard it is for archeologists who find a few pieces of an artifact to draw conclusions as to the use of an ancient object.

Experiment References

Created by Gloria Hoffner. For this program Kelley Smith of Sterling Healthcare and Rehabilitation in Media, PA, built a "sea monster" from a large cardboard box, plastic pipe, and fabric. While under construction and after the program, the sea monster was a great source of conversation among residents. This is an example of a way to further enhance the Science for Seniors program.

Discussion

- Do you believe in the Loch Ness Monster?
- What other, similar creatures have you heard of?
- Do you believe there are new creatures still to be discovered in the Earth's oceans?

Further reading suggestions

Gould, Robert Thomas. 1969. *The Loch Ness Monster and Others.* New York: University Books.

Meredith, Dennis L. 1977. *Search at Loch Ness: The Expedition of the New York Times and The Academy of Applied Science.* New York: Quadrangle/New York Times Book Co.

Miller, Connie Coldwell. 2009. *The Loch Ness Monster: The Unsolved Mystery.* Mankato, MN: Capstone Press.

References

Historic-UK. 2010. Genesis Park. The Plesiosaur. Retrieved August 17, 2010. http://www.historic-uk.com/HistoryUK/Scotland-History/Nessie.htm.

Lake Champlain Land Trust. 2008. Champ, the Famed Monster of Lake Champlain. Retrieved May 27, 2008. http://lclt.org/Champ.htm.

Chapter 7 — Plants

Nearly every one of us remembers going outside in the fall to play in the leaves as children. Whether we jumped in a pile of raked up leaves or just stepped on the leaves to hear the crunch. Or maybe as children we picked flowers for our mothers to put in vases, or gave flowers as a gift to loved ones. This chapter explores the science behind plants and how they work. We will discover just how flowers stay alive so long in the vase and we will also learn how leaves change their color.

Flowers

Introduction

Scientists believe the first flowers appeared on the Earth about 140 million years ago.

By definition, a flower is the part of the plant that allows it to reproduce. Flowers reproduce by bulbs, cuttings, and seeds. Some are perennials which do not have to be replanted each year; others are annuals, which must be replanted each year. While most people enjoy flowers for the lovely appearance and wonderful smell, there are edible flowers. These include leeks, chives, garlic, and garlic chives.

Today there are many thousands of flower species around the world. America's favorite flower is the rose. There are about 1.5 billion cut roses sold in the U.S. each year. This is only a small fraction of billions of flowers bought, sold, grown, pressed, and presented every year.

Roses are the most popular selling flower today, but that was not always true. Prior to 1850, roses were not as popular because they didn't bloom very well and were hard to grow in greenhouses. For these reasons they were limited to being a spring and summer flower. In 1837, the Hermosa became the first rose to be popular with florists. This light pink, short-stemmed rose could be forced to bloom in winter and was used in corsages and small bouquets.

Several other tea roses followed, but it was the American Beauty that captured the hearts of Americans. The rose was imported from France in 1885, deep red in color and long-stemmed. Around 1900, the American Beauty helped roses edge out the carnation as the most popular florist flower.

Trivia

Easy
What does the giving of a single red rose mean?
Answer: Traditionally a single red rose symbolizes love.

Challenging
In folklore what is the meaning of a yellow rose?
Answer: Friendship, joy, and gladness.

Bonus Round
Flowers improve the smell of a room, but do they change the mood of the people in the room?
Answer: Yes, according to The National Gardening Society. They cite a study by Nancy Etcoff from Harvard Medical School and Massachusetts General Hospital. Etcoff studied people between the ages of 25 and 60. She looked at the differences in these people for a week when they had flowers in their homes and a week when they didn't. The results were that, when people had flowers in the home, they were more compassionate, enthusiastic, and happier than when they didn't have flowers in the home.

Video

NOVA First Flower — WGBH Boston — DVD, 2007.
Gardens of the World with Audrey Hepburn — Tribute — DVD, 1993.
Great Gardens of England — Total Content — four DVDs, 2007.

Experiment: How do flowers draw water?

Materials

- Five fresh white carnations or Queen's Anne lace
- Four glass vases (you may use one vase and one color, but several vases if possible for different colors have a more interesting effect)
- A box of food coloring
- Clear water
- A straw
- Knife

Process

Prior to the experiment:

Starting 24 hours before the science program, take four vases filled with water and add one food color to each vase. Make the food color in the vase very dark for best results. Cut the stem of each carnation with a knife on an angle so the capillaries are open. Place one flower in each vase. Keep one carnation in clear water.

During the experiment:

The tips of the carnation petals will turn the color of the water to show how the flower drew the colored water up the stem. Pass the colored and white carnations around the room to the residents. Let them see the color changes and also look closer at the stem of the flower for the tiny tubes that carry water. Cut a small slit in the straw. The straw represents a capillary damaged by freezing temperatures.

Science behind the Experiment

Flowers draw water through capillaries which are tiny tubes, up the stem to the leaves and petals. When flowers are exposed to a cold snap in which the water in the capillaries freezes, the frozen water expands and breaks the capillaries leaving the damaged plant unable to draw water to survive.

Experiment References

Created by Gloria Hoffner.

Discussion

- Who loves to garden?
- What was your first garden?
- What is your favorite flower?

Further reading suggestions

Cresson, Charles. 1993. *Charles Cresson on the American Flower Garden*. New York: Prentice Hall.
Orhbach, Barbara Milo. 1990. *A Bouquet of Flowers*. New York: C.N. Potter.
Torstar Books. 1986. *Flowering Plants*. New York: Torstar Books.

References

Jones, Steve. 2004. Rose Ecstasy. American Rose Society. July/August.
U.S. Department of Agriculture. 2007. Floriculture and Nursery Yearbook. Retrieved January 20, 2008. http://usda.mannlib.cornell.edu/usda/ers/FLO-yearbook/2000s/2007/FLO-yearbook-09-28-2007_summary.txt
The California Cut Flower Commission. 2008. Retrieved January 20, 2008. http://www.ccfc.org/.

Trees

Introduction

A sign of fall is the changing colors of tree leaves from green to shades of red, yellow, and gold. For trees, changing colors is a way of preparing for winter.

Trees draw water from the ground and carbon dioxide from the air. They turn these materials into glucose, a kind of simple sugar, and oxygen. This conversion process is called photosynthesis. A chemical called chlorophyll makes this process possible and is the reason leaves are green.

As the long days of summer end, trees sense the coming of winter and prepare. The winter will mean shorter days with less water and light available for photosynthesis to occur. As the trees shut down their food processing and live off stored reserves, their leaves lose their green color. As a result, the red, gold, and orange colors that has always been in the leaves, but was covered by the dark green of photosynthesis, become prominent.

There are trees that do not change color with the seasons. They are appropriately called evergreens. These trees usually have needles rather than large leaves. The smaller surface gives these trees greater resistance to changes in heat and humidity. Evergreens are able to photosynthesize all year long so they do not change color.

A research project in Germany tested the energy levels of a beech tree with broad, flat leaves, and a Norway spruce tree, an evergreen with needles. The study revealed the beech tree conducted photosynthesis for 176 days while the Norway spruce's photosynthesis process lasted 260 days.

Trivia

Easy
What part of the United States experiences the most fall foliage color?
Answer: The Eastern United States because of the large number of deciduous trees and the change of seasons.

Challenging
What do trees and bananas have in common?
Answer: Bananas like trees have chlorophyll. As the banana ripens, the chlorophyll breaks down and the yellow color comes through. Once picked, bananas have no defense from oxygen in the air and a chemical process called oxidation causes the fruit to turn brown.

Bonus Round
Are all leafy trees structured the same?
Answer: No. There are two basic leaf patterns. On a monolayer tree, (such as a sugar maple), leaves are arranged so that no leaf covers or shades another leaf. In a multi-layer tree (such as an oak) the leaves are above and below other leaves on the tree. On such a tree upper leaves tend to be smaller to prevent over-shading in the tree.

Video

Show Me Science: Ancient Tree — Modern Wonder — TMW Media Group — DVD, 2007.
Show Me Science: Ecology — Tree Top Insects — TMW Media Group — DVD, 2007.
The Oldest Trees on Earth — J. David Productions — DVD, 2005.

Experiment: Why do leaves change color?

Materials

- Fresh leaves
- Baby food jar
- Aluminum foil or plastic wrap
- Rubbing alcohol
- Paper coffee filters
- 10" x 13" baking pan
- Hot water
- Tape
- Pen
- Plastic knife
- Clock or timer

Process

Gather together two or three fresh green leaves from several different trees. Chop up the leaves and place them in the jars making sure to label the jars with the names of the trees.

Next add enough rubbing alcohol to the jars to cover the leaves. Cover the jars with aluminum foil or plastic wrap and place the jars in the baking pan with one inch of water at about 125 degrees.

Keep the jars in the water about an hour making sure to swirl the jars every five minutes. Keep the water around the jars hot.

Cut the coffee filters into strips, Place one end in the jar and the other end taped to the lid of the jar. The alcohol will travel up the filter carrying along the colors of the leaves. Different colors will go different distances up the filter.

Science behind the Experiment

Leaves are green because they have a chemical called chlorophyll. During the spring and summer, leaves turn water and carbon dioxide into oxygen and glucose. In the winter there is not sufficient light and trees shut down their food production and live on the food stored in warmer months. This shutdown results in leaves turning the color seen in fall.

Experiment References

Science Made Simple. 2008. Why Do Leaves Change Color in the Fall?
    Retrieved August 11, 2010.
    http://www.sciencemadesimple.com/leaves.html.

Discussion

- Who had a tree house?
- Who collected leaves as a child?
- Who remembers raking leaves and jumping into the pile?

Further reading suggestions

Lewington, Anna. 1999. *Ancient Trees: Trees That Live for 1000 Years*.
    London: Collins and Brown.
Little, Elbert, L. 1980. *The Audubon Society Guide to North American
    Trees; Eastern Region*. New York: Knopf: Distributed by Random
    House.
Platt, Rutherford Hayes. 1956. *1001 Questions about Trees*. New York:
    Dodd.

References

Penn State University. 2009. What is a leaf? Penn State University.
    Retrieved August 11, 2010.
    http://www.psu.edu/dept/nkbiology/naturetrail/leaves.htm.

Chapter 8 — Earth Science

The Earth we live on is a truly amazing thing. Scientists have been making discoveries about it since the dawn of time and there are no signs of them stopping anytime soon. The experiments we will be conducting in this chapter are meant to help shed light on some of the phenomena that occurs daily on planet Earth. We will be discussing everything from diamonds to floating rocks to tornados and so much more in between. You will never look at the Earth the same way again.

Volcanoes

Introduction

Volcanoes have been part of the Earth since almost the very beginning of the planet. They are part of the geological process that forms the continents. All of the Hawaiian Islands were formed by lava from volcanoes bubbling up from hot spots in the Earth's crust and creating new landmasses.

There are four types of volcanoes: cinder cones, composite volcanoes, shield volcanoes, and lava domes. Here is how they differ:

Cinder cones are the most common in North America. They are built from particles of congealed lava. When this type of volcano explodes, gas-charged lava is blown into the air where it breaks into small cinders, and also sometimes "volcanic bombs." These bombs are chunks of material that fall to the earth. They can be the size of a fist or as large as a small car. The eruption comes from a single vent. The explosion forms a cone shape with a crater at the summit which is usually no higher than about 1,000 feet.

Composite volcanoes are also some of the world's largest mountains. These include Mount St. Helens and Mount Rainier in Washington, Mount Shasta in California, and Mount Hood in Oregon. They formed when magma from within a reservoir in the Earth's crust pushed through to the surface as lava. This lava flowed from a single crater vent or a cluster of vents near the top of the volcano. As the lava, cinders, and ash flowed out of the volcano vent, they built up the slopes and mass of the volcano.

Shield volcanoes are built slowly from lava flow. The Hawaiian Islands are the results of lava pouring up from the ocean floor in an area geologists refer to as the Ring of Fire, made up of the active volcanoes that dot the lands bordering the Pacific Ocean.

Mauna Loa in Hawaii is the largest active and the largest shield volcano in the world. It stands 13,677 feet above sea level with the top of the volcano located over 28,000 feet above the ocean floor.

Lava dome volcanoes are pockets of lava build-up that form on the side of composite volcanoes. As the lava cools, it hardens and eventually breaks apart with the pieces sliding down the sides away from the dome. An example of this type of volcano is Mount Pelée in the Caribbean Sea.

To geologists, there are no such things as inactive volcanoes. Volcanoes are active when they continuously erupt, such as Mt. Katmai in Alaska. A volcano that has erupted in modern times but appears to be inactive now, is called dormant, such as Mount Hood in Oregon.

When a volcano has been inactive during modern times it is called extinct. However, Mount St. Helen's was considered extinct before its eruption on May 18, 1980. Sixty-one people died in the explosion. It was the first volcanic eruption to result in deaths within the contiguous United States. During the 20th century, worldwide, an average of 845 people each year died as a result of a volcanic eruption.

Volcanoes are unpredictable. As long as lava remains in the Earth under a volcano, there is a possibility of an eruption. On August 29, 2010, after 400 years Mount Sinabung in North Sumatra, Indonesia, erupted. It threw sand and ash a mile into the air and produced lava. The government evacuated about 10,000 residents from the volcano slopes. No one was hurt.

Trivia

Easy
What ancient Italian cities were destroyed by a volcano?
Answer: The eruption of Mt. Vesuvius in 79 A.D. destroyed Pompeii and Herculaneum in Italy.

Challenging
What mythical island civilization was destroyed by a volcano?
Answer: According to the writings of Plato, in 1500 B.C. the island of Atlantis was destroyed by a volcano.

Bonus Round

What is the largest volcano in the solar system?

Answer: Olympus Mons on Mars.

Video

National Geographic — Volcano — National Geographic — DVD, 2003.

Nova: In the Path of a Killer Volcano — WGBH Boston — DVD, 2006.

IMAX Ring of Fire — Vista Point Entertainment — DVD, 2006.

Experiment: How does lava flow from a volcano?

Materials Prior to the program

- Two-liter bottle
- Papier-mâché paste (can be made by mixing flour and water to a consistency of heavy cream)
- Glue
- Newspaper
- Straw
- Paint
- Baking pan

Build a tabletop volcano model using a plastic 2-liter soda bottle and papier-mâché. To do this, attach the empty bottle to a baking pan with strong glue. Next crinkle newspaper around the bottle to form the shape of the volcano. Now cover the entire shape with papier-mâché. After you have the basic shape, take a straw and make ruts on the sides of the volcano to simulate the furrows in the sides of a volcano caused by the lava flows. Allow at least one day to dry. Sometimes it takes two days to dry, depending on the mix of your papier-mâché. Once the volcano model is dry, paint it with acrylic paint. You can use dark grey as the base and red in the lava flow areas. Paint the baking pan green for a land-based volcano or blue to represent an island volcano.

If you prefer, you can buy a volcano building kit at a craft or hobby store. These kits contain a form of modeling clay you mix and then paint.

Make sure you have everything you need before leaving the store — some kits do not include the paint and brushes! If possible, have the residents assist in making the model. If they cannot physically work with the model building materials, perhaps they can watch you as you work. Another idea is to place the finished model to dry in an area that can be viewed by residents. The model must be dry before your volcano program.

Materials Day of Experiment

- Red food coloring
- Baking soda
- Vinegar
- Water
- Balloon
- Glass jar
- Funnel
- Liquid dish soap

Process

Using a funnel, pour warm water into the volcano model until the bottle is about 2/3rds full. Have a resident assist you in this process if possible. Next add two tablespoons of the baking soda, red food coloring, a few drops of dish soap. When you are ready for the eruption, add 1/4 cup of vinegar. The reaction of the baking soda and vinegar produces an eruption colored and made bubbly by the addition of red food coloring and the soap. The warm water helps lift and push the explosion upward. This demonstrates the lava flow from a composite style volcano.

Science behind the Experiment

The reaction of baking soda and vinegar (with red food coloring and soap for extra effect) causes the bubbling and simulates how lava flows out of a volcano.

Experiment References

Teacher Vision. 2008. Build a Volcano. Retrieved January 15, 2008.
    http://www.teachervision.fen.com/chemistry/lesson-plan/335.html.

Discussion

- Who has seen a volcano?
- Have you ever visited a museum exhibit on volcanoes?
- Who has seen a movie about volcanoes and how did it differ from the real science of volcanoes?

Further reading suggestions

Bolt, Bruce A., 1980. *Earthquakes and Volcanoes: Readings from Scientific America*. San Francisco: W. H. Freeman.

Gribbin, John. 1978. *Earthquakes and Volcanoes*. New York: Gallery Books.

Robinson, Andrew. 1993. *Earth Shock: Hurricanes, Volcanoes, Earthquakes, Tornadoes, and Other Forces of Nature*. New York: Thames and Hudson.

References

Kidz World. 2010. The Lost City of Atlantis. Retrieved July 6, 2010. http://kidzworld.com/article/960-history-the-lost-city-of-atlantis.

Ferguson, Rebecca. 2006. *The Handy History Answer Book*. Detroit, MI: Visible Ink Press.

Levy, David H. 1997. *The Nature Company Guides Skywatching*. San Francisco: Time Life Books, 1997.

Tucci, Paul A. and Rosenberg, Matthew T. 2009. *The Handy Geography Answer Book*. Detroit, MI: Visible Ink Press.

USA Today. 2010. Volcano quiet for 400 years erupts in Indonesia. Retrieved August 30, 2010. http://www.usatoday.com/news/world/2010-08-28-volcano-indonesia_N.htm?loc=interstitialskip.

Watson, John. 1997. Volcanoes: Principal Types of Volcanoes. Retrieved July 30, 2010. http://pubs.gov/gip/volc/types.html.

Clouds

Introduction

Clouds, the stuff of beautiful days and daydreams, are formed when cool air is saturated with 100 percent humidity. Each cloud is a collection of trillions of drops of water and/or ice crystals that condense around a small particle of material such as dust, pollen, or volcanic ash.

Clouds float due to wind and air pressure. If these conditions end, clouds will dissolve as droplets and fall at a rate of about 30 feet per hour.

About half of the Earth is covered with clouds at any given moment. Luke Howard, of England, designed the cloud classification system that divided clouds by appearance and distance from the ground.

The shape names are cirrus, a curly cloud; stratus, a layered cloud; and cumulus, a lumpy cloud. By height the designations are cirro, clouds above 20,000 feet and alto, clouds from 16,000 to 20,000 feet. Howard did not create a name for lower clouds.

Most clouds are white in color or dark when a storm is coming, but nacreous clouds form 47 to 56 miles above the Earth and have color. Seen in northern locations such as Alaska and Scotland a couple of hours before sunrise and after sunset, these clouds cause a refraction of sunlight resulting in multiple colors at the edge of the cloud.

Noctilucent clouds form at altitudes of 47 to 56 miles, only during the summer at latitudes of 50 to 75 degrees north and 40 to 60 degrees south. These clouds have a bluish color with flecks of red at twilight. Scientists believe the color may be due to meteor dust.

Trivia

Easy

Do airplanes create clouds?
Answer: Under the right conditions, water vapor from jet airplane exhaust forms contrails that can result in an increase in cirrus clouds.

Challenging

What is the U.S. city with the most clouds?
Answer: It is a tie between Astoria, Oregon, and Quillayute, Washington. Both have 240 days of cloud cover.

Bonus Round

What cloud has been mistaken as a UFO?
Answer: Altocumulus lenticularis is a layered cloud often called the flying saucer cloud. It has also been called a cap cloud and a bishop wave.

Video

Reading the Clouds — Educational Video Network — DVD, 2004.
Visions V, 6: Clouds — YOYO — DVD, 2006.
Clouds Video Quiz (2000) — Sunburst Visual Media — DVD, 2009.

Experiment: How do clouds form?

Materials

- Tray of ice cubes
- Glass jar
- Metal baking dish
- Flashlight
- Dark room

Process

Seat the residents in a room that can be made dark. Place the ice cubes so they cover the bottom of the metal baking dish. Place the dish on top of the glass jar. Wait a few minutes and shine a flashlight through the glass jar.

Science behind the Experiment

The warm air mixes with the cold air coming from the metal tray and forms clouds. If you wait a few minutes more, water drops, like rain, will form on the underside of the metal pan.

Experiment References

Beattie, Rob. 2007. *101 Incredible Experiments for the Weekend Scientist.* p. 51. New York: Metro Books.

Discussion

- Who likes to sit and watch clouds?
- Do you remember a particular shape you saw in the clouds?
- Do you remember watching storm clouds form?

Further Reading Suggestions

Dunlap, Storm. 2003. *The Weather Identification Handbook: The Ultimate Guide for Weather Watchers.* Guilford, CT: The Lyons Press.

Rubin, Louis D. and Duncan, Jim authors and Herbert, Hiram J. Contributor. 1989. *The Weather Wizard's Cloud Book: A Unique Way to Predict the Weather Accurately and Easily by Reading the Clouds.* Chapel Hill, NC: Algonquin Books.

Schaefer, Vincent J. and Pasachoff, Jay, authors, and Peterson, Roger Tory, editor. 1998. *Peterson First Guide to Clouds and Weather,* 2nd edition. New York: Houghton Mifflin Harcourt.

References

Hile, Kevin. 2009. *The Handy Weather Answer Book.* Detroit, MI: Visible Ink Press.

Weather.gov. 2010. National Weather Service. Jet Stream Clouds Retrieved May 12, 2010.
http://www.srh.noaa.gov/jetstream/synoptic/clouds.htm.

Thunderstorms

Introduction

A thunderstorm — a bone-rattling and soaking phenomenon — occurs when warm and cold air masses in the atmosphere meet and become unstable. When surface air warms, it rises up through the cooler air above, cooling off as it goes higher until it is the same temperature as the surrounding air. When there is enough moisture in the warm air and a great enough temperature difference, the clouds will become a combination of strong winds, heavy rain, thunder, lightning, and sometimes hail.

Lightning occurs when positively and negatively charged ions meet. In some cases the negatively charged ions make a path down towards the earth and meet with the positively charged ions, which are closer to the ground. When these charged ions meet, the positively charged ions travel up the path that the negatively charged ions made. This reaction is what causes cloud-to-ground lightning. The most common type of lightning is in-cloud lightning where the lightning occurs within the cloud. Another form of lightning is cloud-to-cloud lightning. In this rare type of lightning, the bolt will arc from one cloud to another. Other types of lightning include: ball lightning, dry lightning, heat lightning, and upper-atmospheric lightning.

Contrary to common beliefs, lightning can strike in the same place more than once. There are reports of people being struck by lightning over three times. Similarly, the Empire State Building is often struck more than once during a thunderstorm.

Thunder is one of the byproducts of lightning. A bolt of lightning has a temperature of 100,000 degrees; this is about five times the temperature of the sun. The loud bang that we hear is caused by the superheated air expanding at the speed of sound around the lightning bolt. Even though we see the lightning before we hear the thunder, they are actually occurring at the same time. The speed of light is about 186,282 miles per second. The speed of sound is about one mile in five seconds. You can tell how far away a storm is from your location by counting the number of seconds between a flash of lightning and the following thunderclap.

There are about 44,000 thunderstorms on the Earth each day, a total of about 16 million each year. On average a thunderstorm covers an area of about 15 miles in diameter and lasts about 30 minutes.

Trivia

Easy
What famous American statesman and scientist experimented with lightning?
Answer: Ben Franklin

Challenging
What manmade objects are used to ground lightning in structures?
Answer: Lightning rods.

Bonus Round
How much energy is in a single lightning strike?
Answer: The energy from one bolt of lightning can power a 100-watt bulb for over three months.

Video

Understanding Weather: Storms — Phoenix Learning Group — DVD, 2008.
Earth Science Series: Changes in Weather — Educational Activities — DVD, 1999.
Seashore Spirits — Imagecrafters — DVD, 2009. (This has scenes of thunderstorms, not science information about storms).

Experiment: Why do thunderstorms form?

This experiment will demonstrate the way the cold and hot air masses mix in the atmosphere. The mixing, in the atmosphere, may result in a thunderstorm. This is a visual representation of the air mixing only — not the storm.

Materials

- Clear plastic container (shoebox shape works best)
- Hot water to fill the plastic container about 3/4 full
- Red and blue food coloring
- A clear plastic cup that will allow the contents to freeze without cracking, and access to a freezer.

Process

Prior to the experiment:
Freeze blue water in the clear cup.

During the experiment:
Place all materials on a table or a movable cart. Put the frozen cup of blue water in the plastic container of hot water. The blue water-filled cup will sink to the bottom of the container and blue-colored water will slowly seep out of the cup. Now add drops of red food coloring to the surface of the water in the container. Allow the residents to watch what slowly happens.

Science behind the Experiment

The blue represents a cold front; the red represents heated air. When they mix and form purple tinted water, this demonstrates how warm and cold air mixes in the upper atmosphere to form thunderstorms.

Experiment References

Weather Wiz Kids. 2010. Make a Thunderstorm. Retrieved July 12, 2010. http://www.weatherwizkids.com/experiments-make-thunderstorm.htm.
Modified by Gloria Hoffner.

Discussion

- Were you ever caught in a thunderstorm?
- Have you seen lightning strike something on the ground?
- Who likes to watch a rainstorm?

Further reading suggestions

Galiano, Dean. 2003. *Thunderstorms and Lightning. The Weather Watchers Library*. New York: Rosen Publishing Group.

Graf, Mike. 1998. *Weather Channel Lightning and Thunderstorms*. New York: Simon Spotlight.

Redmond, Jim and Redmond, Rhonda. 2001. *Thunderstorms: Nature on the Rampage*. Chicago, IL: Heinemann Library.

References

Hile, Kevin. 2009. *The Handy Weather Answer Book*. Canton, MI: Visible Ink Press.

NASA. 2010. Tornadoes, Lightning, Thunderstorms...Nature's Most Violent Storms. Retrieved July 22, 2010. http://www.nasa.gov/om.brochures/tt.htm.

Salem, Tom. 2010. How Does Lightning and Thunder Form? Retrieved July 21, 2010. http://www.weatherquestions.com.

Weather Questions.com. 2008. What Causes Thunderstorms? Retrieved July 21, 2010. http://www.weatherquestions.com/What_causes_thunderstorms.htm.

Tornados

Introduction

The exact cause of tornadoes is still a mystery. Scientists believe tornadoes begin as slowly spinning cloud systems that, as an ice skater spins faster as she pulls her arms closer to her body, pick up speeds after a funnel is formed.

They can last from a few minutes to an hour and can have a diameter of up to one mile. The most extreme tornados have wind speeds up to 300 miles per hour and can stretch up to two miles in diameter.

Tornados are rotating columns of air that are in contact with both the surface of Earth and either a cumulonimbus or cumulus cloud. These columns can cause either minor damage or devastate an area.

Tornados occur in many parts of the world, but they are most frequent in the United States, with Oklahoma the hardest hit.

Each year in America there are an average of 1,200 tornados which result in about 70 fatalities and 1,500 injuries. The most dangerous month for tornadoes in the United States is May, with an average of 329 incidences, while February is the safest month, with an average of about three occurrences.

The wind speed of a tornado ranges from 30 to 70 miles per hour, but can reach up to 300 miles per hour. Usually dark grey in color, they can also be white, blue, or even red depending on the composition of the funnel and the sunlight reflecting off the funnel.

A landspout is a weak tornado but can still cause major damage to property and deaths. Their danger lies mainly in that the can produce strong winds. Landspouts usually occur during fair weather.

Dust devils are clouds of dust formed by warm air rising on dry and clear days. They can rise as high as 5,000 feet in the air and reach wind speeds of 60 miles per hour. A steam devil is a weather event that occurs mainly in the Arctic, and sometimes in the Antarctic, when cold air passes over warm water resulting in whirlwinds of steam. They can also occur in hot springs, or above a power plant's smokestack.

Tornados also occur over water; these are called waterspouts. These generally happen during fair weather and are generally less severe than their land counterparts. A tornadic waterspout is a waterspout that occurs during a thunderstorm, these are more severe than fair weather waterspouts.

Trivia

Easy
True or false — tornados do not occur near lakes, rivers, or mountains?
Answer: False. A tornado swept up and down a 10,000-foot mountain near Yellowstone National Park.

Challenging
Do tornadoes always turn counterclockwise?
Answer: Usually tornadoes rotate counterclockwise in the Northern Hemisphere and clockwise in the Southern Hemisphere. However, there are occasionally clockwise rotating tornadoes in the north and super cells that generate both clockwise and counterclockwise tornadoes in the same storm.

Bonus round
True or false — Tornados can occur over water?
Answer: True. Tornadoes formed over warm water are called waterspouts. Waterspouts can travel onshore and damage coastal areas.

Video

Mega Disasters: Tornado Alley — A & E Home Video — DVD, 2009.
National Geographic: Tornado Intercept — National Geographic Video — DVD, 2006.
Twisters: Nature's Deadly Force — VCI Video — DVD, 2006.

Experiment: How do tornados form?

Materials

- Masking tape
- Two empty clear two-liter soda bottles
- Water
- Optional — You can buy a plastic Tornado Tube — used to connect the two soda bottles for about $4.99 in most toy stores. Website: http://Tornadotube.net

Process

Fill one bottle halfway. Connect the bottles with the Tornado Tube or secure the two bottles together with masking tape. Let the water run from the top bottle to the bottom bottle. If the water flow doesn't form a .ex, you can start one by moving the bottles in a circular motion.

Science behind the Experiment

When water flows through a restricted spot, such as the neck between the bottles, it creates a vortex which is similar to the appearance of a tornado. The same thing may happen in the drain of a bathtub.

Experiment References

TornadoTube.net. Purchase information: Telephone: (978) 745-1788; email: tornadotube@verizon.net

Discussion

- Who was in a tornado?
- Who lived in a tornado area?
- How does real tornado differ from the one shown in *The Wizard of Oz*?

Further reading suggestions

Bluestein, Howard B. 1998. *Tornado Alley: Monster Storms of the Great Plains*. New York: Oxford University Press.

Grazulis, Thomas P. 2001. *The Tornado: Nature's Ultimate Wind Storm*. Norman, OK: University of Oklahoma Press.

Rosenfeld, Jeffery O. 1999. *Eye of the Storm: Inside the World's Deadliest Hurricanes, Tornadoes and Blizzards*. New York: Plenum Trade.

References

Hile, Kevin. 2009. *The Handy Weather Answer Book*. Canton, MI: Visible Ink Press.

NASA. 2010. Tornadoes, Lightning, Thunderstorms...Nature's Most Violent Storms. Retrieved July 22, 2010. http://www.nasa.gov/om.brochures/tt.htm.

Earthquakes

Introduction

Earthquakes are generally caused by two things: movement on the boundaries of tectonic plates or movement at the faults which naturally occur in the tectonic plates. The release of stored elastic strain energy at any location is what causes the movement that we feel when an earthquake occurs. Elastic strain energy is the term used to describe the pressure caused by moving tectonic plates or faults.

There are eight major tectonic plates and a few dozen minor tectonic plates which are constantly in motion. When one plate slips above or below another or side-by-side in a horizontal motion the result is an earthquake. Most of the time the plates move slowly side by side. This can be a movement of a few inches or several feet.

Earthquakes are also caused by movements at the faults within tectonic plates. These faults are broken into three main classifications: normal, thrust and strike-slip. Normal and thrust earthquakes cause examples of dip-slip where there is vertical motion. Strike-slip earthquakes cause horizontal movement. Normal faults occur where the crust is being extended, thrust faults occur where the crust is being shortened, and strike-slip earthquakes occur when the two sides of the fault slip by one another. The east African rift is an example of the result of a normal earthquake. Two examples of what occurs due to a thrust earthquake are the Andes and Himalayan Mountains. A strike-slip earthquake is what caused the Dead Sea to form

Earthquakes occur not only on the Earth, but on any active planetary body. NASA has evidence of moonquakes.

Earthquakes that occur under the sea cause tsunamis. They occur about every six years somewhere in the Pacific Ocean. In 2004, tsunamis in the Indian Ocean killed about 238,000 people as the ocean waters rushed onto the land causing sudden and massive flooding. Tsunamis have also hit the United States. In 1964, a tsunami in Prince William

Sound located off the coast of Alaska hit the shore with a 220-foot high wave.

In 2011 there was a disastrous earthquake on Japan's coastline, which caused a massive tsunami. The earthquake, known as the Great East Japan Earthquake, occurred on March 11, 2011. This earthquake was a magnitude 9.0 caused by an undersea megathrust. This earthquake moved the Earth on its axis somewhere between four and 10 inches.

Trivia

Easy
What was the biggest earthquake to hit the United States?
Answer: San Francisco earthquake of 1906 was 8.3 on the Richter scale, killed 3,000 people, and left over 300,000 homeless.

Challenging
What us the strongest earthquake ever measured?
Answer: It struck Chile on May 22, 1960, measured 9.5 on the Richter scale, killed two thousand, and left over two million homeless.

Bonus Round
What earthquake on record took the most lives?
Answer: An earthquake in 1556 in Shaanix, China, killed more than 830,000 people.

Video

Nature Tech — Earthquakes — A & E Home Video — DVD, 2007.
NOVA — Earthquake, the Science behind the Shake — WGBH Boston — DVD, 2007.
NOVA — Killer Quake! (1994) — WGBH Boston — DVD, 2006.

Experiment 1: What causes an earthquake?

Materials

- 12-inch flower arranging foam
- Six-inch pile of dirt
- Large cooking sheet or pan
- Object for cutting foam

Process

Cut a zigzag line in the foam and break in half. Allow residents to see how the two parts can rub together, simulating the earthquake. Tell the residents that the earth is made up of tectonic plates. Explain that the cut in the foam is an example of where two tectonic plates meet. Now place the foam together on the pan. Place a small pile of loose dirt on the foam. Move the two pieces against each other and allow dirt to fall through the crack just as it does in a real earthquake. Slide one foam piece under the other so that they are on top of one another.

Science behind the Experiment

This experiment simulates three types of earthquakes caused by faults: a strike slip earthquake, a thrust earthquake, and a normal earthquake. A strike slip earthquake is an earthquake that occurs when the two sides of a fault rub against each other on a horizontal plane. This type of earthquake is simulated by the residents rubbing the two pieces of foam together. A thrust earthquake occurs when adequate pressure is put on the fault to cause one of the sides to rise. This earthquake is generally associated with a magnitude eight earthquake or more. This is simulated by the residents when they push one piece of foam under the other. The last type of fault earthquake is a normal earthquake. This occurs when one of the sides drops slightly. This earthquake usually has a magnitude of seven or less. As the name hints, this is the most common type of fault earthquake. This earthquake is simulated by the dirt falling through the cracks.

Experiment 2: How does an earthquake feel?

Materials
Table large enough for all participants to sit around
A five-pound exercise weight

Process
Gather residents around a table. (Do not let them see the weight.) Tell them they are going to experience the sensation of being in an earthquake. Have everyone put their hands on the table and close their eyes. Then drop the weight.

Science behind the Experiment
The movement of the Earth's tectonic plates or the faults in the tectonic plates creates a transfer of energy which shakes the ground and can be felt by anyone within the range of the seismic energy.

Experiment References
Johnson, Bill and Francek, Mark. 2010. My Teacher Caused An
    Earthquake. Retrieved August 17. http://www.educationworld.com/
    a_curr/science/esdemo/esdemo0001.shtml.
    This experiment was modified by Gloria Hoffner as follows: I used flower arranging foam rather than Styrofoam so the darker material would be better seen by residents with low vision. I used handheld exercise weights rather than a bowling ball so residents in wheelchairs would feel the sensation in their hands when the weight hit the table rather than dropping a weight on the floor.

Discussion
- Who has been in an earthquake?
- Have you seen news reports about earthquakes?
- Did you ever see a movie about an earthquake?

Further reading suggestions
Bolt, Bruce A. *Earthquakes.* 1988. New York: W. H. Freeman.

D.S. Halacy. 1974. *Earthquakes: A Natural History.* Indianapolis: Bobbs-Merrill.

Simon, Seymour. 2002. *Danger Earthquakes*. New York: Seastar Books.

References

Earthquake.usgs.gov. 2010. Earthquakes with 50,000 or More Deaths. Retrieved August 26, 2010.
http://earthquake.usgs.gov/earthquakes/world/most_destructive.php

Ferguson, Rebecca. 2006. *The Handy History Answer Book*. Detroit: MI: Visible Ink Press.

Tucci, Paul A. and Rosenberg, Matthew T. 2009. *The Handy Geography Answer Book*. Detroit, MI: Visible Ink Press.

Erosion

Introduction

Erosion is caused by wind, ice, and/or water moving across soil and carrying away rock and soil.

The Earth has experienced five ice ages with the last one ending about 670 million years ago. During the ice ages, huge glaciers scoured the earth, moving rocks and soil and reshaping the surface of the planet. Glaciers which retreated between 14,000 and 7,000 years ago formed the Great Lakes.

One of the best examples of water erosion is the Grand Canyon. The Grand Canyon is about a mile deep, over 20 miles wide, and over 250 miles long. The Grand Canyon was formed by the Colorado River cutting a path through the rock for thousands of years.

The river, mudslides, rock falls, and wind still affect the Grand Canyon. Erosion removes about a half a ton of sediment from the canyon every day. This process will continue as long as the river winds through the canyon.

Wind erosion caused the U.S. tragedy called The Dust Bowl. This phenomenon began with the worst drought in U.S. history in 1934. High temperatures, hot winds, and lack of rain combined in mid-April of 1934 and caused dust storms. These storms had winds of 40 to 50 miles per hour and created clouds of soil out of the soil that had covered the landscape in Texas and Oklahoma. A second severe dust storm occurred the following month. As a result of the two storms, more than 650 million tons of topsoil blew off the Great Plains.

Dust covered areas in New Mexico, Colorado, Texas, Oklahoma, and Kansas. The storms killed crops, clogged farm machinery, and killed both livestock and people who ingested the dirt.

Believing the dust storm was due to over farming of the land, President Roosevelt had the civilian corps plant a 100-mile wide zone from Canada to the Texas Panhandle, using over 200 million trees. This along with other conservation methods and return of the rain, allowed grass to grow on the plains and prevented future dust storms. He also began to educate farmers on soil conservation and anti-erosion techniques such as crop rotation, strip farming, and contour plowing. By 1938 the amount of dust blowing was decreased 65 percent.

Beach erosion, the removal of sand to deeper locations in the water by the movements of the water in the ocean, is an ongoing problem. Many coastal communities spend millions of dollars each year replacing sand washed away by the ocean.

Trivia

Easy
Can anything be done to stop beach erosion?
Answer: No. Sand can be replaced but no one can hold back the ocean.

Challenging
How serious is the problem of beach erosion?
Answer: The U.S. Environmental Protection Agency estimates between 80 and 90 percent of the coastal shores lose a few inches up to several feet of beach every year.

Bonus Round
What are sand dunes?
Answer: Sand dunes are formed when sand taken away by the ocean waves is carried back to the beach by the wind. Dunes build slowly and eventually become home to plants which stabilize the dune.

Video

Weathering, Mass Wasting and Erosion — Educational Video Network — DVD, 2004.

All about Weathering and Erosion — Schlessinger Media — DVD, 2000.

Physical Geography Series: Weathering and Erosion — Time Media Group — DVD, 2008.

Experiment 1: What causes erosion?

Materials

- Three 10" x 13" clear baking pans
- Pitcher of water
- Three cups of sand
- Styrofoam cup
- Tissue
- Hairdryer

Process

Place sand in each pan. In two of the pans, make a mountain shape out of the sand. In the third pan spread the sand evenly across the entire pan. Make a pencil-sized hole in the bottom of the Styrofoam cup. Keep your finger over the hole to prevent the water from pouring out while you fill the cup.

Next, hold the cup over the pan filled with smooth sand and let the water drip out. Do the same over one of the pans with the mountain shape. You may need to repeat the process several times to see lines form as a result of the water pushing through the sand.

For the remaining pan, cover the sand mountain with tissue. Then drip the same amount of water over this pan.

Science behind the Experiment

This shows how water wears away soil in a process called erosion. The tissue on the mountain in the third pan represents trees and plants. Soil covered with vegetation will have less water erosion.

Experiment 2: What results from wind erosion?

Materials

- Three 10" x 13" clear baking pans
- Pitcher of water
- Three cups of sand
- Styrofoam cup
- Tissue
- Hairdryer

Process

Place sand in each pan. In two of the pans, make a mountain shape out of the sand. In one of those pans, cover the sand mountain with tissue. In the third pan spread the sand evenly across the entire pan.

Aim the hairdryer at each pan with the setting on low (do this facing the hairdryer away from the residents to avoid blowing sand onto the residents).

Science behind the Experiment

The hairdryer demonstrates how wind erosion affects the soil. The tissue on the mountain in the second pan represents trees and plants. Soil covered with vegetation will have less wind erosion.

Experiment 3: How do glaciers change the surface of the Earth?

Materials

- Frozen ice in an irregular shape
- Flower pot of dirt
- One 10" x 13" clear baking pan

Process

Form the dirt into a mountain shape. Slide the ice down the side of the dirt. Show the residents how the ice picks up and moves dirt as it travels down the mountain shape.

Science behind the Experiment

The irregularly shaped ice in this experiment represents a glacier. Glaciers, along with running water and wind are responsible for some of the reshaping of the earth. As glaciers move they carve out paths across the Earth's surface, leaving behind valleys, depressions, and large rocks.

Experiment References

Experiment #1, #2

Singleton, Glen. 2007. *501 Science Experiments*. Heatherton, Australia: Hinkler Books Pty Ltd.

Experiment #3

Created by Stephen Hoffner-McCall, first place school science fair project, 2000.

Modified by Gloria Hoffner.

Discussion

- Has anyone ever been to the Grand Canyon?
- Has anyone ever seen beach erosion?
- Do you remember stories about the dust bowl during the Great Depression?

Further reading suggestions

Foder, R.V. 1983. *Chiseling the Earth: How Erosion Shapes the Land.* Hillside, NJ: Enslow.

Mattern, Joanne. 2006. *Weathering and Erosion and the Rock Cycle.* New York: PowerKids Press.

May, Julian. 1972. *The Land is Disappearing*. Mankato, MN: Creative Educational Society.

References

Damery, Doug. 2004. Formation of the Great Lakes. Retrieved August 22, 2010.
    http://www.emporia.edu/earthsci/student/damery1/gl_form.html.

Ferguson, Rebecca. 2006. *The Handy History Answer Book*. Detroit, MI: Visible Ink Press.

Hile, Kevin. 2009. *The Handy Weather Answer Book*. Detroit, MI: Visible Ink Press.

Island Beach NJ. 2010. Island Beach Park and Sand Dunes. Retrieved August 22, 2010 from http://www.islandbeachnj.org/Nature/physical/dunes.html.

Scientific American. 2008. What Causes Beach Erosion? Retrieved August 22, 2010. http://www.Scientificamerican.com/article.cfm?id=what-causes-beach-erosion.

Teacher Scholastic. 2010. Erosion — The Grand Canyon. Retrieved August 22, 2010. http://teacher.scholastic.com/dirtrep/erosion/canyon.htm.

Magnets

Introduction

A magnet is an object that is made up of materials that create a magnetic field that has both a north and south. In ancient times, the Greeks and Chinese discovered lodestones were a natural material that could attract small pieces of iron.

Magnets were originally used by travelers because they always point to the northern and/or southern poles. The magnets are used in a compass which is made of a magnetic needle that will either align itself to the northern or to the southern direction of the Earth's magnetic field. The needle is held in a container marked with 360 degrees. By reading a compass users knows what direction they are traveling.

Today magnets are found in everyday situations, such as holding memos and photos on refrigerators, and exotic applications, such as using magnets as a form of space propulsion. NASA and MSE Technology Applications in Butte, Montana, are working together to create a plasma rocket system that works with magnets. This proposed system uses plasma as fuel, which would be regulated by a magnetic nozzle. Using this fuel system a trip to Mars would take three months rather than the eight months with a conventionally powered rocket.

Trivia

Easy
Do magnets work in space?
Answer: Yes. Magnets remain magnetized because of the arrangement of their atoms.

Challenging
Can you de-magnetize a magnet?
Answer: Yes. If you hit the ends of the magnet with a hammer it will destroy the ordering in the magnet.

Bonus Round

What can make the magnetic strip on your credit card stop working? Answer: The strip contains magnetic particles with encoded information. A magnet placed on a magnetic strip destroys the information patterns and causes the strip to stop working.

Video

Modern Marvels: Magnets — A & E Home Video — DVD, 2009.
The Earth is a Giant Magnet — TMW Media Group — DVD, 2008.
Adventures in Science: The Amazing Magnet — Early Advantage —
    VHS (no date).

Experiment: Do magnets work through other objects?

Materials

- Two magnets (small plain magnets and/or magnet wand found in toy stores work best)
- Clear vase with smooth sides
- Paper
- Water

Process

Place a magnet at the bottom of a vase of water. Now place a second magnet on the outside of the vase. Ask the residents: will the magnet be attracted to the second magnet through both the water and the vase? Slide the outside magnet up the side of the vase. The inside magnet will be attracted to the magnet and drawn up through the water.

Remove the magnet from the water and dry it off. Place the magnets on each side of a sheet of paper. Ask the residents if the think the magnets will work through the paper. Slide one of the magnets down the paper so residents can see both moving together.

Science behind the Experiment

Both times the answer is yes because the attraction of magnets is so strong it will work through other materials including water, solids, and gas. The electromagnetic force travels even through the vacuum of space.

Experiment References
    Created by Gloria Hoffner.

Discussion

* Did anyone ever work with magnets?
* Do you remember having toys with magnets?
* Did you study electromagnetic force in school?

Further reading suggestions

Livingston, James D. 1996. *Driving Force: The Natural Magic of Magnets.* Cambridge, MA: Harvard University Press.
Riley, Peter D. 1999. *Magnetism.* New York: Franklin Watts.
Tiner, John Hudson. 2003. *Magnetism.* Mankato, MN: Smart Apple Media.

References

Cool Magnet Man. 2010. What is Magnetism? Retrieved July 19, 2010. http://www.coolmagnetman.com/magattr.htm.
Gunderson, P. Erik. 1999. *The Handy Physics Answer Book.* Detroit, MI: Visible Ink Press.
Stenger, Richard. 2000. Plasma power could usher in human travel to Mars. Retrieved July 19, 2010. http://archives.cnn.com/2000/TECH/space/06/15/plasma.rocket/index.html.

Rocks

Introduction

There are three types of rock that make up the Earth: igneous, sedimentary, and metamorphic.

There are thousands of variations of igneous rocks. Granite, one of the best-known variations of igneous rocks, is often used for countertops. Granite forms from molten material within the Earth.

Sedimentary rock is formed by a slow build up and compression of layers of rock particles, minerals, and even skeletons of microscopic organisms. One of the most common sedimentary rocks is sandstone.

Metamorphic rocks, including marble and slate, are formed when sedimentary rocks are changed by heat and pressure. One of the most famous buildings, the Taj Mahal is made from marble.

Rocks are different from minerals in that a rock can be a combination of several minerals. Minerals are defined by four things: they must be found in nature, have no organic parts, contain the same chemical make-up wherever it's located, and its atoms are composed in a regular pattern.

Aluminum is the most common mineral. It comprises over eight percent of the Earth's crust and is always found in combination with other minerals. Aluminum is used in cookware, beverage cans, electrical cable, and aerospace projects.

Trivia

Easy

What is the Rock of Gibraltar?
Answer: It is a limestone mountain located in southern Spain and used as a British air base.

Challenging

What is fool's gold?
Answer: Iron pyrite. It is a pale yellow color and has a metallic luster that is often mistaken for gold. True gold can be recognized because it is heavier and softer than fool's gold.

Bonus Round

Where in the United States can you dig for diamonds?
Answer: On government land in Murfreesboro, Arkansas, for a fee you can dig for diamonds and keep whatever you find. The largest diamond found at the site since 1972 was 16.37 carets.

Video

Rock and Mineral (DK Eyewitness DVD) — DK Children — DVD, 2006.
Eyewitness: Rocks and Minerals — DK Publishing — DVD, 2007.
Smithsonian Gems and Minerals — Eastman Kodak Company — VHS (no date).

Experiment: Can a rock float?

Materials

- Pumice stone
- Brick or granite
- Clear bowl of water large enough to hold both rocks

Process

Hold up the brick and the pumice stone. Ask the residents to vote on if either the brick or pumice will float. Then place the rocks one at a time in the water.

Science behind the Experiment

The brick will sink because it is heavier than the water it displaces. The pumice will float because it is lighter than the water it displaces. Pumice is made from volcanic magma and contains small amounts of trapped air.

Experiment References

Singleton, Glen. 2007. *501 Science Experiments. #270.* Heatherton, Australia: Hinkler Books Pty Ltd.

Discussion

- Did anyone have a rock collection?
- Did anyone ever dig for rocks in the backyard?
- Did anyone ever save a smooth pebble from a pond or lake as a special keepsake?

Further reading suggestions

Dixon, Dougal. 1992. *The Practical Geologist: The Introductory Guide to the Basics of Geology and to Collecting and Identifying Rocks.* Whitby, ON: Fireside.

Fardon, John. 2009. *The Complete Guide to Rocks and Minerals.* Leicester, England: Hermes House.

Plummer, Charles (Carlos) and Carlson, Diane. 2006. *Physical Geography.* 11th edition. Columbus, OH: McGraw-Hill Science/Engineering/Math.

References

Busbey III, Arthur B.; Coenraads, Robert R. and Willis, Paul. 1997. *The Nature Company Guides to Rocks and Fossils.* New York: Time Life Books.

Carnegie Library of Pittsburgh. 1997. *The Handy Science Answer Book.* Farmington Hills, MI: Visible Ink Press.

Sedimentary Rock

Introduction

There are three basic types of sedimentary rocks. The clastic, such as sandstone, is formed by weathering and debris. Chemical sedimentary rocks form when dissolved materials are pulled out of the rocks. Two examples are rock salt and some limestone. The third kind of sedimentary rock is organic sedimentary rocks such as coal and limestone which are formed by the compression of animal and plant debris.

Sedimentary rocks can undergo natural events and become metamorphic rocks. This occurs when sedimentary rocks are transformed by heat and pressure. Some are shaped by man-made forces but most changes are the result of billions of years of sedimentary buildup being compressed, heated, and twisted by the kinds of powerful earth processes that made the mountains.

Under the surface of the Earth are large deposits of water, oil, and other minerals. When too much water or oil is pumped out of an area of land, the land can sink due to the absence of the liquid that was supporting the land. Large areas of land may slowly sink because of this.

Smaller areas, but still enough to capture houses or cars are called sinkholes. This happens when a small area of ground suddenly drops several feet. These can occur when water has washed away rocks supporting the land to form an underground cavern. If the cavern collapses, the land caves in. This usually happens in areas with large limestone deposits because limestone is easily washed away by water.

Trivia

Easy

Where can you find sedimentary rock?
Answer: These rocks can either be found at the bottom of water, such as a lake, and also on land.

Challenging

Can land be lower than sea level?
Answer: Yes, if the movement of the Earth has pushed down areas of land. An example in the United States is Death Valley in California.

Bonus Round

Why is it that sedimentary rock is the only rock which has fossils?
Answer: The organism is fossilized when it becomes stuck between layers material which is being deposited, for example, at the bottom of a lake. The pressure of material that is deposited later and chemical reactions cause a fossil to form.

Video

Real World Science: Rocks and Minerals — Mazzarella Media — DVD, 2007.
Physical Geography II: Collecting Rocks and Minerals — TMW Media Group — DVD, 2008.
Rock Finders — Thinkeroo — VHS, (no date).

Experiment: How do sedimentary rocks form?

Materials

- Tall clear vase
- Gravel
- Dirt
- Rocks
- Water
- Sand

Process

Before the experiment:
Fill the glass vase with water. Slowly drop in a mix of sand, gravel, and rocks. Allow the materials to settle and the water to clear. Repeat the process. Drain the water and allow the mixture to dry.

During the experiment:
When it dries, remove it from the vase and allow the residents to see the hardened layers. You will be able to snap the new rock and reveal the different layers.

Science behind the Experiment

Sedimentary rocks forms as layer upon layer builds up. The rock can be snapped because the sand layer is the weakest point in the rock.

Experiment References

Experiment by Gloria Hoffner based on information provided by the Delaware County Institute of Science, Media, PA.

Discussion

- Did you ever skip rocks?
- Why are sedimentary rocks the best kind to skip?
- Did anyone ever find a shiny rock and keep it as a souvenir of a trip?

Further reading suggestions

Tucker, Maurice E. 2011. *Sedimentary Rocks in the Field: A Practical Guide*. Hoboken, NJ: Wiley.

Silvestru, Emil. 2008. *The Cave Book (Wonders of Creation)*. Green Forest, AR: Master Books.

Oxlade, Chris. 2011. *Metamorphic Rocks (Let's Rock)*. Mankato, MN: Heinemann Raintree.

References

Busbey III, Arthur B.; Coenraads, Robert R. and Willis, Paul. 1997. *The Nature Company Guides to Rocks and Fossils*. New York: Time Life Books.

Carnegie Library of Pittsburgh. 1997. *The Handy Science Answer Book*. Farmington Hills, MI: Visible Ink Press.

Geology.com. 2010. Sedimentary Rocks. Pictures Characteristics, Textures and Types. Retrieved August 21, 2010. http://geology.com/rocks/sedimentary-rocks.shtml

Go Visit Hawaii. 2007. Hawaii Black Sand Beaches. Retrieved January 24, 2012. http://www.govisithawaii.com/2007/08/hawaii-black-sand-beaches/.

Franklin Institute. 1998. How Sedimentary Rock is Formed. Retrieved August 21, 2010. http://www.fi.edu/fellows/fellow1/oct98/create/sediment.htm.

Tucci, Paul A. and Rosenberg, Matthew T., 2009. *The Handy Geology Answer Book*. Detroit, MI: Visible Ink Press.

Metals

Introduction

Mankind has been mining metals from the Earth since about 6000 B.C. Today there are 86 known metals. In the discovery of the most popular metals, the oldest is gold. Artifacts made of gold have been found as early as the 4th millennium B.C. Copper was discovered in 4200 B.C., silver in 4000 B.C., lead in 3500 B.C., tin in 1750 B.C., iron in 1500 B.C. and mercury in 750 B.C.

The first two metals to be used by the ancient civilizations of Mesopotamia, Egypt, Greece, and Rome were gold and copper. They were used as jewelry and coins.

In the 21st century, metals can be found throughout our homes, places of work and recreation. Some examples include aluminum in soda cans and, in the form of aluminum hydroxide, in carpet backing and fire extinguishers.

Silicon is used in computers, cell phones, and solar energy cells. Copper is in the electrical wiring and in water pipes. Iodine is found in soap and lead is found in batteries.

Trivia

Easy
What center of electronics in named for a metal?
Answer: Silicon Valley in California.

Challenging
What minerals have been named when referring to the ages of humankind?
Answer: Copper Age, Bronze Age, and Iron Age.

Bonus Round

What are the most popular metals in airplanes and what is replacing them?

Answer: Aluminum and titanium. These are being replaced by carbon fiber in the latest models.

Video

Sheet Metal Shearing and Bending — Society of Manufacturing
    Engineers — DVD, 1997.
Sheet Metal Stamping Presses — Society of Manufacturing Engineers —
    DVD, 1997.
History — Modern Marvels: Brooklyn Bridge —A & E Television
    Networks — DVD, 2008.

Experiment: Why do your feet feel colder on metal than on a rug?

Materials

- Metal plate large enough for a foot (could be an aluminum cookie sheet)
- Throw rug
- Volunteer with bare feet

Process

Ask for a volunteer. Have the volunteer remove his/her shoes and socks. Ask the volunteer to place his/her foot (feet if it's a large metal plate) on the metal. Next, ask the volunteer to place his/her feet on the rug. Have the volunteer say which feels cooler.

Science behind the Experiment

Both the metal plate and the rug are actually at room temperature. The metal plate is a better conductor of heat so it draws heat faster from the body. Because your foot is losing heat faster on the pan, your foot will feel warmer resting on the carpeting, which doesn't conduct heat as fast.

Experiment References
Created by Gloria Hoffner based on information in:
Gunderson, Erik, P. 1999. *The Handy Physics Answer Book*. p. 163.
    Detroit, MI: Visible Ink Press.

Discussion

- Who has worked with metals?
- Did anyone ever visit or work in a mine?
- How many metal objects can we find in this room?

Further reading suggestions

Kou, Sindo. 2002. *Welding Metallurgy,* 2nd edition. Hoboken, NJ:
    Wiley-Interscience.
Lippold, John C. and Kotecki, Damian, J. 2005. *Welding Metallurgy and
    Weldability of Stainless Steels,* 2nd edition. Hoboken, NJ: Wiley-
    Interscience.
Messler, Robert W. Jr. 2010. *The Essence of Materials for Engineers*.
    Sudbury, MA: Jones and Bartlett Publishers.

References

Cramb, Alan W. 2010. A Short History of Metals Retrieved August 20,
    2010. http://neon.mems.cmu.edu/cramb/Processing/history.html
Jindal Stainless Steel. 2010. Know Stainless Steel.
    http://www.jindalstainless.com/stainlesssource/know-stainless-
    steel/faq.html.

Diamonds

Introduction

Diamonds are the Earth's hardest natural substance. They are crystalline carbon formed under extreme pressure. They are categorized as precious gems because they have three qualities: beauty, durability, and rarity.

Diamonds are usually found in Africa, Siberia, India, and Australia. Other locations include Brazil, Russia, and Venezuela. Diamond mines are usually located near volcanic areas and rivers. One diamond producing area in the U.S. is Crater of Diamonds State Park in Arkansas. It is the only diamond-producing site in the world open to the public.

Usually colorless, there are rare blood red diamonds. Bort and carbonado, which are an inferior quality diamond, are less attractive and are used by industry as drill bits, saws, abrasives, and polishers.

Most diamonds are used in jewelry. A well-known diamond in the United States is The Taylor-Burton Diamond. Weighing 69.42 carats, the pear shaped diamond was given and named by actor Richard Burton as a gift for actress Elizabeth Taylor. He bought it for $1,100,000. After his death in 1979, Taylor sold the stone for $2.8 million and donated the money in Burton's memory to a hospital in Biafra.

Trivia

Easy
How are diamonds weighed?
Answer: By caret. A caret is 1/142 of an ounce.

Challenging
What is the largest cut diamond?
Answer: The Great Star of Africa is the largest cut diamond in the world. It was cut from the Cullinan Diamond, discovered January 25, 1905,

which was the world's largest weighing 3,106 carets. It was found in the Premier Diamond Mine in South Africa.

Bonus Round

What is used to cut a diamond?

Answer: Another diamond is the only substance on Earth hard enough to cut a diamond.

Video

History — Modern Marvels: Diamond Mines — A & E Television
    Networks — DVD, 2008.
Nature: Diamonds — Questar — DVD, 2004.
Blood Diamonds — History Channel, A & E Home Video — DVD,
    2007.

Experiment: How do gemologists test for genuine diamonds?

Materials

- Diamond
- Water
- Fingertip

Process

Clean a diamond ring. Wet a fingertip with water. Place your finger on the diamond and feel the attraction to the water.

Science behind the Experiment

A thoroughly clean diamond has the ability to almost magnetize water. Thus the stone will be attracted to water.

Experiment References

Based on information in: Carnegie Library. *The Handy Science Answer Book.* p 131. 1997. Carnegie Library of Pittsburgh, Farmington Hills, MI: Visible Ink Press.

Discussion

- Who remembers their first diamond?
- What was your favorite piece of diamond jewelry?
- Did you ever give someone a diamond?

Further reading suggestions

Dickinson, Joan Younger. 1965. *The Book of Diamonds: Their History and Romance from Ancient India to Modern Times*. New York: Crown Publishers.

Michelsen, Solfus S. 2010. *A Journey through West Africa in Search of a Million Carets of Diamonds (Vol. 1)* Seattle, WA: CreateSpace.

Peltzman, Ronne and Grant, Neil — editors; Casebourne, Sue — artwork and maps. 1980. *Diamonds, Myth, Magic and Reality*. New York: Crown.

References

Busbey III, Arthur B.; Coenraads, Robert R., and Willis, Paul. 1997. *The Nature Company Guides to Rocks and Fossils*. New York: Time Life Books.

Arlecchino Jewles. 2010. The World's Ten Most Famous Diamond. Retrieved August 30, 2010.
http://www.studiosoft.it/JewelryWorlds10.htm.

Minerals in Food

Introduction

Minerals, made of metals and other inorganic compounds, are as essential to bodily functions as vitamins. Although it is possible to get most of the minerals we need from dietary supplements, the best source of minerals comes from eating a healthy diet.

We need a large set of minerals to stay healthy. The minerals are divided into major minerals and minor minerals.

Major minerals are considered major because they are required by the body in doses of 100 mg/day or greater; i.e. greater than 0.01% of body weight. Major minerals are calcium, phosphorus, potassium, sodium, chloride, magnesium, and sulfur.

Minor minerals are required by the body in amounts of less than 100 mg/day; i.e. less than 0.01% of body weight. They are also called trace minerals or trace elements. Minor minerals are chromium, cobalt, fluoride, zinc, selenium, silicon, boron, iron, copper, iodine, manganese, molybdenum, nickel, arsenic, and vanadium.

Minerals serve many purposes in our bodies. Here are some examples. Calcium is the most common and abundant mineral in the body and is found primarily in the bones and teeth. A small but absolutely essential amount of calcium is found in the blood and soft tissue. Iron is essential for metabolism, DNA synthesis, growth, healing, immune function, and reproduction. Its best-known function is it's role in hemoglobin, which transports oxygen through the blood and muscles. A lack of iron can lead to anemia.

Magnesium is essential for energy production, protein formation, and cellular division. It is as important as, if not more important than, calcium and phosphorus. Sodium and potassium work together to maintain the electrical charge of the cell, which is critical for nerve function and muscle contraction. Potassium deficiency results in fatigue and muscle weakness.

Trivia

Easy
Who invented breakfast cereal?
Answer: The American Seventh Day Adventist in the 1860s in Battle Creek, MI.

Challenging
Who created corn flakes?
Answer: Keith Kellogg in 1894. He was a physician and a member of the American Seventh Day Adventists.

Bonus Round
Is too much iron harmful to humans?
Answer: Yes for people with hemochromatosis, a disease in which the intestines absorbs too much iron from the diet.

Video

Classic Cereal Commercials from the 50's and 60s: Collector's Edition Volume 1 — Video Resources New York — VHS (no year).

Experiment: Why is there iron in food?

Materials
- Plastic bag that will seal shut
- Cup of cereal (Total, Special K, and others high in iron work best)
- Water
- Strong magnet (tell the hardware store you need a strong magnet and explain your experiment)
- Magnifying glass

Process
Crush the cereal and place it in a bag with water. When the cereal is completely mushy, run the magnet on the outside of the bag. The magnet will pull tiny bits of iron towards the side of the bag for viewing. You may need a magnifying glass for residents with low vision to see the iron specks.

Science behind the Experiment

Iron is in the guardrails on highways, in breakfast cereal, and vitamins. The iron in cereal is food grade metallic particles. Why is iron in food and inside humans? It is actually a component in the proteins that carry oxygen through the body and iron also regulates cell growth.

Experiment References

Steve Spangler Science. 2010. Eating Nails for Breakfast. Retrieved August 20, 2010.
   http://www.stevespanglersceince.com/content/experiment/00000034.

Discussion

- What is your favorite breakfast food?
- As a child, did you pick your breakfast food for the prize inside the box?
- How do you get adequate minerals in your diet

Further Reading Suggestions

Clydesdale, Fergus, M. 1985. *Iron Fortification of Foods (Food Science and Technology)*. Waltham, MA: Academic Press.

References

Amodro, Almee. 2010. Why does my body need iron? Retrieved August 20, 2010. http://health.families.com/blog/why-does-my-body-need-iron.

Emax Health. 2010. Too Much Iron in Your Body is Harmful. Retrieved August 20, 2010. http://www.emaxhealth.com/39/3091.html.

Massachusetts Institute of Technology. 2005. Optimizing Your Diet: Best Foods for Specific Minerals. Retrieved February2, 2012. http://web.mit.edu/athletics/sportsmedicine/wcrminerals.html

Chapter 9 — Everyday Chemistry

In your lifetime you might have wondered why certain things like soap work so well to remove stains from clothing. Or you might have wondered why metal rusts or how paper is made. All of these are examples of everyday chemistry. We will study these and a few more in this chapter. You will never look at Coca-Cola the same way when you learn it is not just a delicious drink, but also very helpful in everyday life!

Soap

Introduction

Soap was first created in Italy in 600 A.D. with animal fats. The Spanish improved the product in 700 A.D. with the inclusion of olive oil. Soon after, the French added perfume to the soap and became world leaders in the process.

During the 1800s America families made soap by boiling household fats with grease and lye from wood ashes to make a harsh yellow-colored soap.

Soap is made in two ways: the kettle method or the continuous process.

In the kettle method, fats, oils, and lye (sodium hydroxide) are placed in a kettle and heated. Salt is added and the mixture is re-heated. It then cools with the upper 70 percent soap and the lower 30 percent a mix of soap, glycerin, and remaining fats. If animal fats are used in making soap, the soap will not lather in cold weather. Vegetable oils in the soap will make the soap lather.

The continuous process was developed in the 1930s. This method is done in a factory with stainless steel tubes. Molten fat is pumped into one end of the column, while at the other end water at high temperature (266°F) and pressure is introduced. This splits the fat into two components: fatty acid and glycerin. These are pumped out continuously as more fat and water enter.

The purified fatty acids are mixed with alkali to form soap. Other ingredients such as abrasives and fragrance are also mixed in. The hot liquid soap may be then whipped to incorporate air. The soap is then cooled and hardened in a large block. The entire continuous process, from splitting to finishing, can be accomplished in several hours.

The final step is cutting and packaging the soap into bars. Most toiletry soap undergoes additional processing called milling. The cooled soap is fed through several sets of heavy rollers (mills), which crush and knead it. Perfumes may be added at this time. After the soap emerges from the mills, it is pressed into a smooth cylinder and extruded. The extruded soap is cut into bar size, stamped, and wrapped.

Trivia

Easy
What happens if you leave a bar of soap in the water?
Answer: It dissolves. This happens because the liquid in water breaks apart the grease in the soap.

Challenging
How much soap does the average American use each year?
Answer: About 25 pounds.

Bonus Round
How are granulated soaps made?
Answer: Soap is pumped in liquid form out of a high tower and, as it falls as a mist through a heated chamber, the drops dry into grains of soap powder.

Video

Colonial America — Quick Tips to the History of Daily Life — School Co. — VHS (no date).
A Day in the Life — Colonial Williamsburg Foundation — DVD, 2008.
The Home Electrical Modern Appliances 1950 — Quality Information Publishers Inc. — DVD (no date).

Experiment: How does soap remove dirt from clothing?

Materials

- Laundry soap
- Water in a pitcher
- Basin
- Dirt covered washcloth

Process

On a table place the soap, dirty washcloth, basin, and water in a pitcher. Show the residents the dirty washcloth. Rub soap into the cloth. Next pour water into the basin, add the washcloth, and rub the soap into the cloth. When you see the stains disappear, wring out the cloth, and show the residents.

Science behind the Experiment

Soap works because it lowers the surface tension of water. This allows the water to pass through and break up the molecules of dirt on the cloth. The soap molecules actually surround the dirt and break it up into smaller particles that go into the wash water as it is tossed away.

Experiment References

Created by Gloria Hoffner based on the information in:

Funk and Wagnalls. 1984. *Funk and Wagnalls New Encyclopedia of Science, Vol. 18.* p 1556. Milwaukee, WI: Raintree Publishers Inc.

Discussion

- Did anyone ever make soap?
- Do you remember scrub boards?
- Do you remember wringer washing machines?

Further reading suggestions

Pringle, Patrick. 1953. *How it's made: Stories of the manufacture of everyday things: wool, tea, soap, coal, money, biscuits, oil, carpets, books, etc., etc.* Peoria, IL: Royal Publishers.

Stone, Harris, A. and Seigel, Bertram M. 1968. *The Chemistry of Soap.* Englewood Cliffs, NJ: Prentice-Hall.

Romanelli, Paola. 2002. *Making Soaps.* Cincinnati, OH: North Light Books.

References

Funk and Wagnalls. 1986. *Funk and Wagnalls New Encyclopedia of Science.* Milwaukee, WI: Raintree Publishers.

How Products Are Made. 2012. Soap. Retrieves February 2, 2012. http://www.madehow.com/Volume-2/Soap.html

Rust

Introduction

Rust is formed when oxygen reacts with iron.

It's common to see rust on automobiles. The paint and protective coating on cars protects the surface from rust. However, as you drive, the car is hit by pebbles, rocks, and other items on the road that can nick the paint. Where the paint has been removed rust can form.

The corrosion due to rust will continue until a hole is formed in the car's metal. To slow this process, the rusted area of the car should be cleaned with sandpaper and repainted.

Rust, while annoying, can also be dangerous. A rusted frame in a car can collapse. If this occurs while driving, it may cause a serious accident.

A famous rust disaster happened in Angers, France, in 1850. The rusty cables of the Basse-Chaine Bridge over the Maine River collapsed causing the death of 478 French soldiers.

Trivia

Easy

Can the rusting process be reversed?

Answer: No, this is an irreversible process.

Challenging

What is done to prevent rusting in outdoor weather?

Answer: Metals are treated with a coating, such as paint on cars, to prevent rusting.

Bonus Round

How does stainless steel resist rusting?

Answer: Stainless steel contains a minimum of 10.5 percent chromium. Chromium has a chemical reaction with oxygen in the air and forms a protective chrome-oxide layer on the outside of the metal.

Video

American Industry & Manufacturing History Films, Classic Industries from Logging to Textiles to Steel — Quality Information Publishers Inc. — 33 DVDs (no date).

1943 Steel Production — Quality Information Publishers Inc — DVD (no date).

Modern Marvels: American Steel Built to Last — History Channel — DVD, 1998.

Experiment: Why does metal rust?

Materials

- Three paper cups
- Three cheap blunted iron or steel nails (not galvanized or coated)
- Two tablespoons of table salt
- White vinegar
- Water
- Spoon
- Marker
- Paper towel

Process

Before the experiment:

Prior to the Science for Seniors program, label the cups, salt water, vinegar, and water. Take the cups and the materials to the program.

During the experiment:

At the program, fill the cup marked salt half full with water and add two tablespoons of salt. Stir well to dissolve the salt. Fill the cup marked vinegar half full of vinegar and do the same with water in the final cup. Place a nail in each cup. Show the video.

At the end of the video and before the discussion, take the nails out of the solution and let them sit for about 10 minutes on a paper towel. The longer the nail sits in the solution and the air, the more rust. You might want to do a set prior to the program as an illustration of a nail left for several days in the solutions.

Science behind the Experiment

Rust is a result of oxidation, a chemical reaction that occurs when iron is exposed to moisture and oxygen. Adding salt and vinegar speeds up the rusting process because the chemical combination increases corrosion.

Experiment References

Seek. 2010. Science and Engineering Experiments for Kids. Retrieved August 20, 2010. http://www.msm.cam.ac.uk/SeeK/rustynails.htm.

Discussion

- What is the rustiest thing you have ever seen?
- Did anyone work in an automobile factory making cars out of steel?
- Did anyone work with steel, either making it or using it?

Further reading suggestions

Brandt, Daniel A. 1999. *Metallurgy Fundamentals*. Tinley Park, IL: Goodheart-Wilcox.

McGannon, Harold E., editor. 1964. *The Making, Shaping and Treating of Steel*. Pittsburgh: United States Steel.

Roberts, William L. and Munther, Per. 2011. *Hot Rolling of Steel*. Boca Raton, FL: CRC Press.

References

Corrosion Doctors. 2010. Rust Prevention Tips. Retrieved August 30, 2010. http://www.corrosion-doctors.org/Car/Rust-Prevention.htm.

Dr. Beakman. 2010. Physics in Daily Life. Swings, Bridges and Sopranos. Retrieved August 30, 2010. http://ourentirefamily.com/drbreakman/.

Jindal Stainless Steel. 2010. Know Stainless Steel. It's All About: Stainless Steel. Retrieved August 21, 2010. http://www.jindalstainless.com/stainlesssource/know-stainless-steel/faq.html.

Soda Pop

Introduction

The first marketed soft drinks (non-carbonated) appeared in the 17th century. They were made from water and lemon juice sweetened with honey. In 1676, vendors carried tanks of lemonade on their backs and dispensed cups of the soft drink to thirsty Parisians.

In the late 18th century, scientists started producing artificially carbonated water. In 1767, Englishman Joseph Priestley suspended a bowl of distilled water above a beer vat. Priestley found that water treated in this manner had a pleasant taste, and he offered it to friends as a refreshing drink.

Another Englishman, John Mervin Nooth, improved Priestley's design and sold his apparatus for commercial use in pharmacies. Swedish chemist Torbern Bergman invented a generating apparatus that made carbonated water using chalk and sulfuric acid to produce the carbon dioxide. Bergman's apparatus allowed imitation mineral water to be produced in large amounts. Swedish chemist Jöns Jacob Berzelius started to add flavors (spices, juices, and wine) to carbonated water in the late 18th century.

Coca-Cola Bottling Company is the largest beverage manufacturer in the world offering 500 brands of soda, fruit drinks, teas, and coffees. The company's beginning goes back to 1886 when John Pemberton, a pharmacist in Atlanta, Georgia, made Coca-Cola in his backyard.

In 1886, Pemberton sold about $50 worth of soda at Jacob's Pharmacy in Atlanta, with an annual loss of about $20 on the product. The following year, Pemberton sold his recipe to Asa Candler, another Atlanta pharmacist, for $2,300.

Candler's salesmanship increased the product sales more than 4,000 percent between 1890 and 1900. Candler sold his Coke syrup to soda fountains which made the beverage on site. Soda fountains were a successful selling location for Coke until the 1960s when the fountains began to be replaced by fast food restaurants.

Trivia

Easy
What was the occupation of the inventors of Coke, Pepsi, and Dr. Pepper?
Answer: They were all pharmacists. John Pemberton (Coke), Caleb Bradham (Pepsi), and Charles Alderton (Dr. Pepper).

Challenging
Which came first, Dr. Pepper or Coca-Cola?
Answer: Dr. Pepper-1885, Coca-Cola-1896, Pepsi-1898, R.C. Cola-1905.

Bonus Round
What current beverage company started as Unadulterated Food Corporation?
Answer: Snapple.

Video

Coca-Cola Film History Library — International History of Coke, Soda Pop, and Soft Drinks, Vendo Vending Machines, and More — The Historical Archive — DVD (no date).

Experiment 1: Why can you clean a car battery with a soft drink?

Materials

- Corroded car battery
- Eight ounces of Coca-Cola
- Pan large enough to hold battery

Process

Place the battery on a table in a pan to catch the runoff. Pour the soda over the corroded battery terminals.

Science behind the Experiment

The Coca-Cola works because the mild alkali in Coke and Pepsi dissolves the battery corrosion. Mixing baking soda and water on the battery terminals will also work for the same reasons.

Experiment References

Tipking. 2010. Clean car batteries and neutralize battery acid corrosion on cars. Retrieved August 20, 2010. http://www.tipking.co.uk.3553.html.

Experiment 2: Why do Mentos candies make soda erupt?

Materials

- Pack of Mentos candies
- Eight-ounce bottle of soda (regular or diet but diet will make less mess because it has less sugar)

Process

Place Mentos in a full soda bottle. The mixture will shoot out of the bottle.

Science behind the Experiment

The surface of the Mentos has tiny pits called nucleation sites where carbon dioxide bubbles form once in contact with the soda. When the

Mentos hits the soda, bubbles form all over the surface of the candy and the pressure pushes soda out of the bottle.

Experiment References

Steve Spangler. 2010. Making Science Fun. Mentos Exploding Drink: the Hoax. Retrieved August 20, 2010.
http://www.stevespanglerscience.com/content/experiment/mentos-mix-an-exploding-drink.
Modified by Gloria Hoffner.

Discussion

- Who remembers soda fountains where the soda pop was mixed by hand?
- Did you ever make soda at home?
- How many different kinds of soft drinks can you think of?

Further reading suggestions

Charles, Oz. 1988. *How Does Soda Pop Get Into the Bottle*. New York: Simon and Schuster Books for Young Children.
Tchdi, Stephen. 1986. *Soda Poppery: The History of Soft Drinks in America with recipes for making and using soft drinks plus easy science experiments*. New York: Scribner.
Witzel, Michael Karl and Young-Witzel, Gyvel. 1998. *Soda Pop from Miracle Medicine to Pop Cultural*. Stillwater, MN: Town Square Books.

References

Bellis, Mary. 2010. The History of Coca-Cola: John Pemberton was the inventor of Coca-Cola. Retrieved August 20, 2010.
http://inventors.about.com/od/cstartinventions/a/coca_cola.htm
Coca-Cola. 2010. About the Coca-Cola Company. Retrieved August 20, 2010. http://www.coca-cola.com/index.jsp.
Wikipedia. 2012. Soft drink. Retrieved February 2, 2012.
http://en.wikipedia.org/wiki/Soft_drink.

Paper

Introduction

The first paper on Earth was not made by humans. It was, in fact, made by insects. Wasps chew wood into a pulp they use to make their hives.

For thousands of years humans used tree bark, rocks, blocks of wood, and even animal skins as a writing surface. Paper was invented in China about 2,000 years ago by a man named Ts'ai-Lun. He combined fibers from the inner bark of a mulberry tree with scraps of linen and hemp. The oldest book ever found was located in China in an area called the Caves of the Thousand Buddhas. The book is entitled *The Diamond Sutra* and was published in 868 A.D.

In about 500 A.D., the Mayans of Central America discovered how to make paper from fig tree bark. The first paper mill in the U.S. was built in Philadelphia, Pennsylvania, in 1690. At this time paper was made from linens and rags.

Paper can be made from cloth, trees, cotton plants, cornstalks, wheat straw, hemp, and jute plants. In the United States most paper is made from wood pulp and more recently from recycling of paper products. The use of wood pulp became popular in the U.S. starting in 1869.

The process of cutting down trees for papermaking adds to the pollution released in the atmosphere. Recycling paper into new paper products saves both energy and trees.

According to the U.S. Environmental Protection Agency, every ton of paper recycled would save enough energy to power a house for six months. In addition it will save 7,000 gallons of water, 3.3 cubic yards of landfill space, as well as reduce greenhouse gas emissions by one metric ton of carbon.

Trivia

Easy

What materials are used to make paper products? What is the most common material?

Answer: About half from harvested trees and the remainder is wood fiber from sawmills, recycled newspaper, some vegetable matter, and recycled cloth.

Challenging

How much paper do Americans use each year?

Answer: The United States uses about 85 million tons of paper which is made into more than two billion books, 350 million magazines, and 24 billion newspapers. An average American uses a 100-foot Douglas fir tree in paper and wood products each year.

Bonus Round

How much paper do Americans recycle?

Answer: In 2006 the U.S. recycled about 44 million tons. This is a recycling rate of about 50 percent. Americans recycled about 88 percent of their newspapers and 72 percent of their corrugated cardboard.

Video

EARTH AID: Recycling — V.I.E.W. — DVD, 1994.

Where the Garbage Goes — Fred Levine Productions/Little HardHats — DVD, 1996.

All About Garbage and Recycling — Giaim — DVD, 2008.

Experiment: How is paper recycled?

Materials

- Sponge
- Window screening
- Old picture frame
- Plastic basin large enough to totally immerse frame
- Blender/food processor for making paper pulp
- White felt or flannel fabric the size of the frame or a little larger
- Staples for tacking screen on frame
- Liquid starch optional
- Old newspaper
- Water
- Gallon plastic container

Process

Prior to the experiment:

Make a mold by stretching window screen material over an empty picture frame and stapling it tightly into place.

During the experiment:

At the Science for Seniors program, give each resident some paper to tear up into small pieces. While they are tearing the paper, place your frame in the bottom of your basin and fill the basin with water until it is half-full. Place to the side. After the residents have torn their paper into small pieces, fill the blender halfway with the paper and then fill it the rest of the way with warm water. Run the blender until the paper has turned into a pulp. Make sure no large pieces of paper remain. Do this as many times as needed to create enough pulp to cover the frame, if using liquid starch, make sure to mix it in well.

Pour the pulp into the basin and move the screen side to side to ensure the paper is dispersed evenly over the screen.

The next step is to slowly lift the mold up until it is above the basin. Wait until most of the water has drained from the new paper sheet and inspect the results. If the paper is very thick, remove some pulp; too thin, add more pulp and, in either case, stir the mixture again and re-try with the mold until you have your desired results.

When the mold has stopped dripping, place the fabric over the top of the mold, hold the mold securely with both hands, and carefully turn the frame over on the table. Using a sponge, press out as much water as you can. Lastly, lift the frame away from your newly made paper. Once dry, remove the fabric and you will be left with a sheet of paper.

Science behind the Experiment

Trees contain cellulose fibers and lignin, an organic polymer found in plant tissue. When starting with virgin wood, the chipped tree material is treated with acid or alkaline to dissolve away the lignin, in order to filter out the wood fibers which will be used to hold the paper together.

In recycling, when paper is broken down, each of the wood fibers that make up the paper keeps much of its length. It's the mat of crossed wood fibers that holds paper together. When the paper is recycled too many times, the wood fibers get too short to hold the paper together.

Experiment References

Pioneer Thinking. 2010. Making Homemade Paper in 10 Easy Steps. Retrieved August 22, 2010. http://www.pioneerthinking.com/makingpaper.html. Modified by Gloria Hoffner.

Discussion

- Did anyone work for a paper manufacturing plant?
- Did anyone take part in recycling at home or work?
- Did anyone work or live near logging companies?

Further reading suggestions

Branson, Gary D. 1991. *The Complete Guide to Recycling at Home: How to Save Money, Take Responsibility and Protect the Environment.* White Hall, VA: Betterway Productions.
Goldstein, Jerome. 1979. *Recycling: How to Reuse Waste in Home, Industry and Society.* New York: Schocken Books.
The Earth Works Group. 1989. *50 Simple Things You Can Do to Save the Earth.* Berkeley, CA: Earthworks Press.

References

Answers.com 2012. What are the paper production process steps? Retrieved February 4, 2012. http://wiki.answers.com/Q/ What_are_the_Paper_production_process_steps

Environmental Protection Agency. 2010. Paper Recycling. Retrieved August 22, 2010.
http://www.epa.gov/waste/conserve/materials/paper/basics/index.htm

Ferguson, Rebecca. 2006. *The Handy History Answer Book*. Detroit, MI: Visible Ink Press.

Funk and Wagnalls. 1986. *The New Encyclopedia of Science.* Milwaukee, WI: Raintree Publishers Inc.

U.S. Department of Agriculture. 2008. Making Paper from Trees. Forest Service U.S. Department of Agriculture FS-2. Brochure.

Chapter 10 — Physics All Around Us

You may have never studied physics in your past schooling, but it's never too late to start! In this chapter we will first study subjects like viscosity, the law of universal gravitation, and the law of inertia just to name a few. After we have learned the physics behind these subjects we will conduct experiments to demonstrate how they work.

Viscosity

Introduction

Viscosity, the resistance of an object moving through liquids or gases, is something we seldom think about in daily life. It is, however, a critical factor in how things work in the world around us. This can be shown in three common examples.

First, the automobile. A car needs motor oil to run the engine so that moving parts don't rub against one another and heat up enough to melt the engine. Motor oil thickens on a day with cold temperatures. For this reason, when starting a car on a freezing day, you should allow the car's engine to warm up for a few minutes before driving. Driving the car before the oil is freely moving can damage the engine.

A second example is in the kitchen. When using honey and/or syrup, warming their containers will allow the product to flow more quickly and provide easier use.

A third example is house paint which is a shear-thinning fluid. This means when sitting it starts to gel, but when stirred it thins and can be used on brushes and rollers.

One place we have all experienced the effects of viscosity is when we have been in the water. Water is much more viscous than air. Think about how much more energy it takes to move your hand through water. That is the result of its viscosity.

Trivia

Easy
What country uses the most oil?
Answer: The United States.

Challenging
Who produces the most oil?
Answer: Russia produces about 9.37 million barrels a day.

Bonus Round

How much oil is produced daily around the world?

Answer: 73.5 million barrels.

Video

Speed (IMAX) — Image Entertainment — DVD, 2004.

Core Physics: Classical Physics/Modern Physics — Ambrose Video —
    two DVDs, 2007.

Liftoff: Just a Lot of Hot Air — Science House — Download free science
    videos created by Dan Menelly from
    http://sciencehouse.com/videoscience-experiments.html.

Experiment: How does viscosity affect the speed of objects moving in liquids?

Materials

- Two large microwavable clear pitchers of equal size
- Water
- Several packets of nectar thickening powder such as that which is used to thicken drinks for residents with swallowing difficulties
- Two medium sized rocks
- Microwave

Process

Fill both pitchers ¾ full with water. In one pitcher add several packets of thickener until the water has a consistency of a milkshake. Ask the residents to guess: Will the rock fall at the same speed in both liquids?

Now warm the pitcher with the thickened liquid in a microwave and repeat the experiment.

Science behind the Experiment

Viscosity is the term for resistance of an object moving through gas or liquid. The thicker the liquid the more it resists the object moving through it. This is because there is friction between the object and the thick material. The viscosity of a material decreases as the temperature increases.

Experiment References

Created by Gloria Hoffner based on information from

Funk and Wagnalls, Inc. 1986. *Funk and Wagnalls New Encyclopedia of Science Vol. 21.* p 1785. Milwaukee, WI: Raintree Publishing, Inc.

Discussion

- Do you remember starting a car on a cold winter day?
- Have you ever used syrup right out of the refrigerator?
- How are aerobic exercises different when you do them in a swimming pool?

Further reading suggestions

Dennis, Johnnie T. and Moring, Gary. 2006. *The Complete Idiots Guide to Physics.* Indianapolis, IN: Alpha.

Kuhn, Karl L. 1996. *Basic Physics.* New York: J. Wiley.

Lehrman, Robert L. 2009. *Barron's E-Z Physics.* Hauppauge, NY: Barren's Educational Series.

References

Funk and Wagnalls. 1986. *Funk and Wagnalls New Encyclopedia of Science Vol. 21.* Milwaukee, WI: Raintree Publishing, Inc.

Physics. 2010. Viscosity: The Physics Hypertextbook. Retrieved August 22, 2010. http://physics.info/viscosity.

Herring, Hubert B. 2006. Who Produces the Most Oil? Not Who You Think, published September 17, 2006. *The New York Times.*

eHow.com 2010. How to Start a Car in Winter. Retrieved August 21, 2010. http://www.ehow.com/how_2063947_start-car-cold-weather.html.

Gravity

Introduction

Sir Isaac Newton discovered the Law of Universal Gravitation when he determined that all objects in the universe that have mass are attracted to each other. Newton stated gravity's strength changes as the square of the distance between the masses.

For example, the distance from the center of the earth to the surface is about 3950 miles. An astronaut twice as far from the center of the earth (7900 miles, also 3950 miles above the surface) will feel ¼ of the gravitational pull. Astronauts ten times as far from the center (39,500 miles) will feel only one percent (1/100) of the gravitational pull experienced on Earth.

There is a common misconception that there is no gravity on other planets. But Newton's Law of Universal Gravitation applies to any masses, including you and the moon or you and Mars. For example, a person weighing 110 pounds on Earth will feel the tug of gravity as if they weighed three pounds on the surface of Pluto or 42 pounds on Mars. The difference in the weight you feel is caused because these planets (or dwarf planets) are smaller than Earth. On Jupiter you would feel like you weighed 3498 pounds.

Trivia

Easy

True or false: did Newton really discover the law of gravity when an apple fell on his head?

Answer: True. An apple falling on his head in 1665 started him wondering why objects are attracted to the Earth.

Challenging
What is the center of gravity?
Answer: The center of gravity is the average location of an object's mass.

Bonus Round
How did the Law of Universal Gravitation help with the discovery of Neptune?
Answer: In 1846, French astronomer Urbain Leverrier determined from the orbit of Uranus that there must be another planet beyond Uranus pulling on it. Later that year, Johann Galle, a German astronomer, discovered Neptune less than a degree from where Leverrier calculated the eighth planet would be located.

Video

Squibs Disc 3 — In Force Gravity, Friction and Work — Ignite Learning
    — DVD, 2005.
The Science of Disney Imagineering: Gravity Classroom Edition —
    Disney Educational Productions — DVD, 2007.
Bill Nye the Science Guy: Gravity Classroom Edition — Disney
    Educational Productions — DVD, 1994.

Experiment: Why does a parachute slow you down?

Materials

*   Toy parachute soldiers which can be found in toy stores

Process
    Give each resident a toy parachute soldier with the parachute still wrapped and held in place by the rubber band. Have the residents throw the toy up in the air and watch what happens. Now take one parachute soldier to the front of the room, stand on a chair, and drop the toy with an open parachute for everyone to watch.

Science behind the Experiment

When the parachute is wrapped tight, the force of gravity pulls the toy to the floor. There is little air resistance to counteract gravity. When the parachute is opened, the viscosity of the air opposes the force of gravity and slows the fall to the ground. In a vacuum, where there is no air to cause air resistance, the soldier would fall the same speed regardless of whether the parachute was open or not.

Experiment References

Created by Gloria Hoffner.

Discussion

- Who has ridden on a roller coaster?
- Has anyone ever parachuted?
- Has anyone ever bungee jumped?

Further reading suggestions

Nardo, Don. 1990. *Gravity: the Universal Force*. San Diego, CA: Lucent Books.

Tiner, John Hudson. 2003. *Gravity*. Mankato, MN: Smart Apple Media.

Wheeler, John Archibald. 1990. *A Journey into Gravity and Spacetime*. New York: Scientific American Library.

References

Gundersen, P. Erik. 1999. *The Handy Physics Answer Book*. Farmington Hill, MI: Visible Ink Press.

Fluids

Introduction

Any gaseous or liquid material that can flow is considered a fluid. Water is the most plentiful fluid on the surface layer of the planet. It flows above ground as surface water in rivers, streams, and oceans as well as below the Earth as groundwater or in aquifers. Water is also present in the atmosphere as well as frozen in glaciers.

Water is denser as a liquid than it is as a solid. You can see that because ice floats on the surface of the ocean, lake, or even in your glass of water.

Water condensation occurs when vapor from warm water, which has as great deal of energy, collides against cooler and slower moving molecules in a water container. The water vapor changes to a liquid in the form of water drops that form on the container.

Trivia

Easy
What is the freezing temperature of water?
Answer: 32 degrees.

Challenging
How does evaporation cool our bodies?
Answer: Water molecules in sweat evaporate into the air. The process of evaporation removes heat from the surface of our skin. Without this process our bodies could overheat.

Bonus Round
How do clouds form?
Answer: Warm air rises in the atmosphere and expands. This warm water vapor cools and condenses forming water droplets. The droplets attach themselves to other particles in the air and the result is clouds.

Video

Water — the Great Mystery — Intention Media Inc. — DVD, 2008.

Science World 4A — Water from the Sun 1997 — National Archives and Records Administration — DVD, 2010 (deals with irrigation systems).

Water and Weather — Penguin Productions — VHS, 1987.

Experiment: Why does water spread evenly across a pan?

Materials

* 10" x 13" clear glass baking pan
* A large enough pitcher of water to fill the pan

Process

Start by showing the residents the empty baking pan. Next point out how you are adding water only to the left side of the pan. Ask them to watch what happens. The water will flow until it is level across the pan. Next tell them you will pour water on the right side of the pan and ask them to watch what happens to the water level in the pan.

Science behind the Experiment

All liquids rest at the same level. You cannot make one side higher by adding liquid only to that side. Since water can flow, gravity pulls it until it is flat, which is the lowest energy state.

Experiment References

Created by Gloria Hoffner based on information in:

Gundersen, P. Erik. 1999. *The Handy Physics Answer Book*. p. 121. Farmington Hill, MI: Visible Ink Press.

Discussion

* What was your favorite water hole or place to swim?
* Did you ever play with the only liquid metal, mercury, as a child (and why don't we let children play with mercury any more)?

- Which is the most beautiful waterfall you have ever seen?

Further reading suggestions

Ball, Philip. 2000. *Life's Matrix: A Biography of Water*. New York: Farrar, Straus and Giroux.
Dennis, Jerry. 1996. *The Bird in the Waterfall: A Natural History of Oceans, Rivers and Lakes*. New York: Harper Collins Publishers.
National Geographic Society. 1978. *The Powers of Nature*. Washington, DC: The Geographic Society.

References

Hile, Kevin. 2009. *The Handy Weather Answer Book*. Detroit, MI: Visible Ink Press.

Motion

Introduction

Sir Isaac Newton discovered three laws of motion that govern how objects move.

First is the law of inertia, which states that an object at rest stays at rest and an object in motion stays in constant motion unless and until another force changes that motion.

For example, imagine a hockey puck sitting still on the ice. It will keep sitting there until someone or something hits it. Once set in motion, the puck will continue to slide across the ice until it hits a wall, is struck by a hockey stick or skate, or until the force of friction from air resistance and ice slows and finally stops the puck.

The second law, force, looks at the relationship between the amount of force, the size of the object, and the effect the force has on the object. For example, a grown man pushing a child in a wagon can accelerate faster than a small child pushing a grown man in the same wagon because the grown man can generate more force and what he is pushing is lighter.

The third law is that for every action there is an equal and opposite reaction. An example is the recoil from a gun. The gun pushes the bullet out of the chamber accelerating it to a very fast speed in a very short time. Newton's third law states that the bullet will also exert an equal but opposite force on the rifle, which then collides with your shoulder. The action in this example is the bullet leaving the gun, the equal and opposite reaction is the force of the recoil which the shooter experiences as the butt of the gun collides with the shoulder.

Trivia

Easy
Why do we have seat belts in cars?
Answer: To protect ourselves from the law of inertia. This means when a car is moving forward with speed and stops suddenly, the law of inertia would keep our body moving forward and hitting the windshield. The seatbelt stop the inertia of the body moving forward.

Challenging
Are speed and velocity the same thing?
Answer: No. Speed is the distance an object travels in a certain time, such as 60 miles per hour. Velocity is the speed of an object and the direction it is traveling.

Bonus Round
What is considered to be the fastest moving thing?
Answer: Albert Einstein said the limit in the universe we experience is the speed of light. Physics equations allow for the possibility of objects called tachyons that can never move slower than light, but they are not something that we can sense with our slower-than-light sensors.

Video

The Science of Disney Imagineering Newton's 3 Laws of Motion — Disney Educational Productions — Interactive DVD, 2009.
The Three Laws of Motion — Cerebellum Corporation— DVD, 2004.
Newton's Laws of Motion with Friction — TMW Media Group — DVD, 2008.

Experiment: Why does the Earth continue to rotate?

Materials
- Toy spinning top
- Football

Process
Spin the top. This is an example of the Earth rotating on its axis. Next, throw the football with a spiral.

Science behind the Experiment
The Earth is an example of the law of rotational inertia which states: an object will continue to rotate until an outside force changes its rotation. This means our planet will continue to rotate forever unless there is an outside force that causes it to stop. The top and the football stop their rotations when friction slows the rotation and gravity pulls them to the ground.

Experiment References
Gunderson, Erik P. 1999. *The Handy Physics Answer Book.* p. 78. Detroit, MI: Visible Ink Press.

Discussion

- How does it feel to ride on spinning fair rides?
- Has anyone been in a car accident? What happened?
- Do you remember being pushed or pushing someone on a playground swing?

Further reading suggestions

Lewin, Walter. 2011. *For the Love of Physics: From the End of the Rainbow to the Edge of Time — A Journey Through the Wonders of Physics.* New York: Free Press.

Gianopoulos, Andrea. (Author), Miller, Phil (Illustrator), Barnett, Charles (Illustrator). 2007. *Isaac Newton and the Laws of Motion.* North Mankato, MN: Capstone Press.

Zimba, Jason. 2009. *Force and Motion: An Illustrated Guide to Newton's Laws*. Baltimore, MD: The Johns Hopkins University Press.

References

Gunderson, Erik P. 1999. *The Handy Physics Answer Book*. Detroit, MI: Visible Ink Press.

Chapter 11 — Tall Tales and Science Facts

This chapter is dedicated to the scientist in all of us. In this chapter we will not only explore the science behind popular sayings, such as it's hot enough today to fry an egg on the sidewalk. But we will also discover why our tongues stick to flagpoles in the winter, as well as why we can hear the sea when we place a seashell or a cup to our ear. We will also learn about the man in the moon and the city of Atlantis.

There are many human expressions, stories, and myths in science heard almost every day, but how many of these are true? These are a series of fun experiments to explain the science behind the legends.

Experiment 1: Can you fry an egg on a hot sidewalk?

Materials

- Egg
- Aluminum foil
- Hot, sunny, undisturbed location
- Optional — video camera for recording, if residents cannot observe outside, or a camera to take pictures

Process

Crack an egg on a piece of aluminum foil and place it on a sidewalk or driveway in direct sunlight. Leave for several hours and observe. Optional — take a video or digital camera photos of the experiment in the beginning, mid-day, and after eight hours to show residents who may be unable to come to the location and see the experiment for themselves. Ask residents to vote on whether they think the egg will cook? For fun — ask the kitchen staff as well! Post both votes before the end of the day.

Science behind the experiment

The egg needs a sidewalk temperature of 158 degrees to cook to firmness. In most U.S. locations, sidewalks can reach a temperature of about 145 degrees.

At the Oatman, Arizona, Annual Solar Egg Frying Contest, contestants have 15 minutes to cook their eggs and may use a mirror, a magnifying glass to focus the sun's heat on the egg, and/or aluminum reflectors to increase the cooking temperature. Locations such as Death Valley on the Nevada and California border where the summer temperature reaches over 120 degrees are ideal areas fry your eggs. Low humidity helps the cooking process making states like Arizona ideal states for cooking outside.

The truth of this tall tale depends on when and where you cook the egg. While sidewalks are poor conductors of heat, metal is an excellent conductor of heat. Eggs have cooked in the sunlight on a car hood.

Gloria Hoffner conducted this experiment in the Philadelphia area on a 102-degree day in July. The white evaporated and the yoke cooked a little on the top.

Experiment References

The Library of Congress. 2010. Science Reference Services. Retrieved July 6, 2010. http://www.loc.gov/rr/scitech/mysteries/friedegg.html.

Experiment 2: If you place your tongue on a metal pole on a freezing day, will your tongue freeze to the pole?

Materials

- Popsicles
- Volunteer tongues

Process

Give the residents frozen Popsicles and have them place their tongue gently on the side of the Popsicle. Yes — their tongues will stick briefly.

Science behind the Experiment

The water between the tongue and the Popsicle freezes briefly thus sticking the two together just as a tongue would stick to a metal pole on a freezing cold day. The metal in the pole must be below 32 degrees for the freezing to occur. If your tongue does become stuck, it is best to try and heat the area where your tongue is stuck instead of trying to pull it off.

Experiment References

CCMR. 2006. Metal's thermal conductivity makes your tongue stick in winter. Retrieved August 17, 2010.
http://www.ccmr.cornell.edu/education/ask/index/html?quid=777.

Experiment 3: When you place a seashell to your ear, can you hear the ocean?

Materials

- Large spiral conch shell
- Volunteer
- Coffee cup

Process

Have the volunteers hold the shell against their ears and report what they hear. Pass the shell around to let all the interested residents have a turn to listen. For extra fun, have the residents hold a coffee cup over their ear and report what sound they hear.

Science behind the Experiment

The sound you hear is not coming from the ocean. Instead, it is from the ambient noise from your surroundings. The shell acts like a resonating chamber capturing the ambient noise from around you. Sound waves enter the shell and bounce around creating an audible noise. The louder the ambient sounds around you, the louder the sound of the "ocean" in the shell. This is way the cup also works in producing "ocean sounds."

Experiment References

How Stuff Works. 2010. Why Can You Hear The Ocean When Holding a Seashell to Your Ear? Retrieved August 7, 2010. http://science.howstuffworks.com/question556.htm

Experiment 4: How often is there a blue moon?

Materials

- 10-inch Styrofoam ball
- Pencil
- Two volunteers
- Dark room

Process

Place the Styrofoam ball on the pencil; the ball represents the moon. Give the moon to a volunteer. (The volunteer must be able to move without assistance.) Give the flashlight, which represents the sun, to another volunteer who will stand still at the front of the room and hold the light on the moon at all times. Start with the moon between the volunteer with the flashlight and the audience. The audience will not be able to see the light the sun is shining on the moon. This is what happens during a new moon.

Next, have the volunteer with the moon move to the left of the audience. As the moon moves, the audience will be able to see more and more of the lighted surface. When the moon is directly to the left of the audience, the moon is in the first quarter.

The moon should keep moving until it is behind the audience. The full face of the moon will be bright like a full moon. (If a clever resident puts up a hand to block the sunlight, you will have a lunar eclipse.) As the moon continues around the room, the audience will be able to see less and less of the lighted surface until the moon comes back to the front again as another new moon.

Science behind the Experiment

The initial position, with the moon between the sun and the audience is a new moon. The moon to the left is the first quarter. In the back it is a full moon. On the right it is the third quarter. The reason we have phases of the moon is because the angle between the sun, earth, and moon changes as the moon goes around the earth, just as the Styrofoam moon moved around the audience.

The term Blue Moon does not refer to the color of the moon. Rather it means two full moons occurring within one month. This happens about every 2.72 years. It will never happen in February because there must be 29.53 days between the two full moons. The next Blue Moon (at the time this was written) will be August 31, 2012.

The moon can appear blue at any time due to material in the atmosphere, such as smoke from large forest fires or dust from a dust storm.

A harvest moon is the full moon closest to the autumn equinox in September. Folklore says a harvest moon gives farmers extra time to bring in their crops. A hunter's moon is the full moon after a harvest moon.

Experiment References

Chaulk. 2010. Phases of the Moon Experiment. Retrieved August 18, 2010. http://chaulk.richmond.edu/education/projects/webunits/cycles/moonexperiment.html.

NASA. 2009. Blue Moon on New Years' Eve. Retrieved August 18, 2010. http://science.nasa.gov/science-news/science-at-nasa/2009/29dec_bluemoon/.

Carnegie Library of Pittsburgh. 1997. *The Handy Science Answer Book.* Farmington Hills, MI: Visible Ink Press.

Experiment 5: Why do we see a face on the moon?

Materials

- 10" x 13" clear baking dish
- Small rocks
- Flashlight
- Dark room
- Flour

Process

Fill the baking pan with flour. Have the residents gently toss rocks into the flour. Remove the rocks. Turn off the lights and shine the flashlight at various spots on the pan. Ask the residents what they see.

Science behind the Experiment

The moon reflects sunlight giving it a white glow. The dark areas of the moon are basins formed by the impact of meteors and comets.

The Man on the Moon is actually the largest crater on the moon. It is named the Imbrium Basin and is 700 miles wide. We see it as a human face because our brains are wired to see human faces more than any other shape. Doris Tsao, a neuroscientist at the University of Bremen in Germany, discovered that groups of cells in the temporal region of the brain are attuned to detect faces.

Experiment References

Svoboida, Elizabeth. 2007. *Faces, Faces Everywhere. The New York Times*: February 13, 2007.

Moon shape experiment created by Gloria Hoffner.

Experiment 6: Why do we wear dark-colored clothing in the winter and light-colored clothing in the summer?

Materials

- Three pans filled with crushed ice or snow
- Three pieces of felt: a white, a blue and a black piece, each cut to fit over a pan
- Sunny windowsill
- Video camera if residents cannot observe during the experiment

Process

Place the filled pans in direct sunlight at the start of the day. Either take pictures and/or show residents. Take a second set of pictures and/or show residents the status of the experiment at lunchtime. At the end of the day, before sundown, take a photo and/or show the residents what has happened to the ice/snow in the pans. The black will melt the fastest, followed by the blue, and then the white.

Science behind the Experiment

Dark colors absorb more light and therefore more heat energy than light colors. The sunlight turns into heat and thus melts the snow. Pans with dark material melt faster than pans covered with light colored material.

Experiment References

Physics Central. 2010. Physics in the Snow: Snowy Colors. Retrieved June 14, 2010. http://www.physicscentral.com/experiment/physicsathome/snow.cfm.

Experiment 7: Could volcanic gases have killed the people of Atlantis?

Materials

- Glass jar
- Funnel (must cover jar opening when funnel is upside down)
- Balloon
- Baking soda
- Vinegar

Process

Place baking soda in the jar. Add a ¼ cup of vinegar and quickly place the funnel with the balloon attached to the funnel neck upside down over the jar. The balloon will inflate.

Science behind the Experiment

During a volcanic eruption, a volcano sends out carbon dioxide gas. The gas created in this experiment from the interaction between the baking soda and the vinegar is also carbon dioxide, and can be "seen" when the balloon inflates. Carbon dioxide is not a problem unless there is a lot of it. It's the gas that's in soda pop and we create carbon dioxide when we use food to create energy in our bodies.

Archeologists believe poisonous volcanic gases, many more dangerous than carbon dioxide, quickly overcame the people of the ancient city of Pompeii in Italy whose preserved bodies were discovered lying trapped under volcanic ash just where they fell. A combined volcano and earthquake event may have also doomed the people of Atlantis.

The mystery of the City of Atlantis has captured human imagination since 350 B.C. when Plato wrote of the island in the Atlantic Ocean that sank under the sea in a single day.

Scholars have studied the possibility and have searched for clues to Atlantis for over 200 years. In the late 1800s Ignatius Donnelly wrote a book called *Atlantis, the Antediluvian World* claiming it was a real place destroyed by a natural disaster. In the 1960s, Angelos Galanopoulos reported that around 1500 B.C. a volcano destroyed the island of Santorini in the Mediterranean, which could be a model for the story of Atlantis.

Experiment References

Created by Gloria Hoffner.

Experiment 8: Can you ever find the end of the rainbow?

Materials

- Clean CD
- Sunny window
- Table
- Flashlight in dark room

Process

Place the CD label side down on a clean sunny windowsill or table near the window. As the sunlight or light from a flashlight hits the CD, a rainbow image will appear.

Science behind the Experiment

Light is a mixture of colors. The grooves in the CD will split the light so it appears as individual colors as in a rainbow.

Rainbows are formed when you stand with the sun behind you at less than 42 degrees above the horizon and rain drops in front of you. As the sunlight enters the raindrops, the wavelengths of color are refracted at different rates to produce bands of different colors. It usually seems like you can never reach the end of the rainbow because the ends of the light refraction you can see are somewhere in the distance. The ends seem to move away from you as you move toward the rainbow.

Under the right circumstances you can see the ends of the rainbow continue in their arc until they form a complete circle. This is most easily done with a garden hose. If the sun is in exactly the right place, the bottom of the rainbow is at your feet. *You* can be the end of your rainbow, even if you can't always see it.

References

The Naked Scientists. 2010. Kitchen Science Experiments. Colours in CDs. Retrieved August 17, 2010. http://www.thenakedscientists.com/HTML/content/kitchenscience/exp/colours-in-cds/.

Hile, Kevin. 2009. *The Handy Weather Answer Book*. Detroit, MI: Visible Ink Press.

Chapter 12 — Ways to Establish Ongoing Interest in Science

The Science for Seniors program may spark a desire in residents and staff to seek new ways to incorporate science discoveries into every day life. Here are a few long-term ideas.

Create a Science for Seniors library. Seek donations of books from schools and family members. Series of books you may want to include:

- Eyewitness Books published by DK Children.
- Handy Science Answer Books by Visible Ink Press.
- Scientific American Library series by Scientific American.

Build a collection of science themed videos for use by residents who due to illness cannot leave their rooms. Suggested titles:

- Eyewitness — produced by Penguin Group USA.
- The Best of Beakman's World — produced by Sony.
- Bill Nye the Science Guy DVD collection — produced by GIAIM Americas.
- The Science of Imagineering — produced by Disney Studios.

Give Science for Seniors materials a permanent place in your activity room. Keep supplies for last minute program changes and needs. These can include vinegar, baking soda, 10" x 13" clear baking pan, clear vases, measuring cup and spoons, and water pitchers. It is helpful to have a large whiteboard easel for printing fun facts or to use to keep score as residents guess the outcome of a science experiment.

Make a Science for Seniors binder to record the experiments you have done. This makes it easier to remember what you did last month or last year and is a quick reference when you are asked to repeat an experiment and/or program. This is also a good place to store articles you may read and want to try as a current event science program.

Plant a butterfly garden near a large open window with a nearby seating area. This will allow residents to observe flowers, butterflies, and insects, etc. If possible include bird feeders, birdbaths, and an outdoor thermometer to help residents feel a connection with nature.

Contact local clubs including: gardening clubs, and rock collectors, bird watchers, astronomy groups, Girl and Boy Scouts, 4-H, etc. Let them know your residents are interested in being involved in nature projects that they might be working on.

Stretch Science for Seniors into other ongoing groups at your facility. Example — Garden club members can conduct the acid rain experiment. The craft group can make bird feeders and props for programs. The book reading club can report on a nature book they read last month and include that topic as a Science for Seniors program. The facility cat and dog can take part in the animal experiments.

When possible, add props to set the mood for the Science for Seniors program. A prop, such as building a dinosaur, a submarine, or a Loch Ness monster from cardboard, can spark interest and ongoing discussion among residents. A poster of space photos, flowers, or rocks can be used to advertise the next Science for Seniors program and be re-used the day of the program as decorations.

Handy websites for quick references

News and Current events

- Science Friday — National Public Radio program with current events in science — sciencefriday.com
- Scientific American magazine — www.scientificamerica.com

Fun general websites

- How to do just about anything — eHow.com
- How stuff works — howstuffworks.com

Government Agencies

- National Aeronautic and Space Administration — NASA.gov
- National Oceanic and Atmospheric Administration — NOAA.gov
- National Institutes of Health — nih.gov
- U.S. Department of Agriculture — usda.gov
- U.S. Forest Service   us.fe.fed.us
- U.S. National Park Service — NPS.gov
- U.S. Environmental Protection Agency — EPA.gov
- U.S. Geological Survey — www.usgs.gov/

Private companies

- Animal Planet — animal.discovery.com
- Bill Nye the Science Guy — www.billnye.com
- Discovery Channel — discoverychannel.com
- Geology — Geology.com
- Globe Program — www.Globe.gov
- McGraw-Hill Encyclopedia of Science and Technology — www.mhest.com/
- Public Broadcasting System — www.PBS.org
- Smithsonian Institute — www.si.edu/
- The Science Channel — science.discovery.com
- The History Channel — www.history.com
- The National Geographic Society — www.nationalgeographic.com

Places to buy materials

- Books, VHS, and DVDs — Amazon.com
- Books, VHS, and DVDs — Ebay.com
- Books, VHS, and DVDs — Barnes and Nobel.com

- Rent and/or buy DVDs — Blockbuster.com
- Rent DVDs — Netflix.com

Special items you may want to buy

- Home Astro Planetarium by Sears. About $60. Projects stars and planets. Great in a dark room.
- Uncle Milton Star Theater 2 sold by Uncle Milton. About $30. Projects a planetarium view in a room — must be a small and windowless dark room. Find these two and other space image projectors at www.bixrate.com under planetarium toys.
- Sand and Water Wheel sold toy stores. To demonstrate water power.
- A globe — simple 12-inch is fine. I like an inflatable globe because when you talk about the amount of water covering the planet, etc., it is lightweight and easy for all residents to examine and pass around.
- Magnifying glass
- Set of magnets of various shapes and strengths. Available in craft, hardware, and toy stores.
- Quality flashlight.

Epilogue

I sincerely hope you and your residents have enjoyed the Science for Seniors programs in this book. My hope is that the topics in this book will spark an interest in learning more about the world in which we live and produce lively discussions among staff, residents, and family members.

May you, your staff, and your residents discover the curious scientist within each of us. When you go beyond the book and devise Science for Seniors experiments of your own, please consider sharing them by contacting us at Idyll Arbor.

About the Author

Science for Seniors grew out of Gloria Hoffner's experiences running Science for Seniors programs combined with her extensive readings of the latest scientific research on aging. As she describes it, at the heart of the book is the idea that we are never too old to learn!

Gloria is an award winning activity professional and a career journalist. After a long career with the *Philadelphia Inquirer*, Hoffner pursued her lifelong interest in science and began working in senior communities as the owner of "Guitar with Gloria."

She created her trademarked program, "Science for Seniors" in 2007 and has presented it in facilities throughout Pennsylvania, Delaware, New Jersey, and Maryland. In 2010, Science for Seniors was awarded first place in Best Practice division of the National Certification Council of Activity Professionals. The award recognized Science for Seniors as the most outstanding new activity program design among retirement, assisted living, personal care, long-term care, and adult day center facilities.

Hoffner is also a frequent speaker at national and statewide conventions for professionals in the healthcare, activity, and certified therapeutic recreation fields. She is a contributing editor to *Creative Forecasting* magazine and a columnist for the website About.com.

She lives in Media, Pennsylvania, with her husband Jim.